Unless otherwise indicated, all scripture quotations are taken from the New King James version of the bible.

Standing on my Healing: From Tainted to Chosen

ISBN-10: 194698258X
ISBN-13: 9781946982582

Copyright © 2017 by Alicia E. Diggs

Publishing, Editing and Cover by: DYmondFYre Global Publishing

Photo Credits: Derek Palmer Photography, L.A. Photography and Okeeze Artography

Printed in the United States of America.

All rights reserved under International Copyright Law.
Contents and/or cover may not be reproduced in whole or in part in any form without the express written consent of the publisher, DYmondFYre Global Publishing.

Standing on my Healing: From Tainted to Chosen

By Alicia E. Diggs

Table of Contents

My Dedication..

Introduction..

Reflection 1- Tee and Lee...1

Reflection 2 - Rocky's Double Trouble..............................5

Reflection 3- The Greatest Love of All.............................12

Reflection 4- Making Adult Decisions.............................15

Reflection 5- I Adore Him..21

Reflection 6- Young, In Love and Blind..........................25

Reflection 7- What a Wonderful life, Right?...................29

Reflection 8- Hungry, Sick and Tired.............................33

Reflection 9- I'm Not Ready..37

Reflection 10- Just Tired..41

Reflection 11- The Older Man...45

Reflection 12- Time to Leave Old Things Behind................55

Reflection 13- Whirlwind...61

Reflection 14- A New Chapter in Life................................65

Reflection 15- Back to Philly, Again...................................67

Reflection 16- My High School Sweetie..............................71

Reflection 17- Listen to 'The' Voice....................................75

Reflection 18- Don't Marry this Man!.................................79

Reflection 19- The Shock of my Life...................................83

Reflection 20- HIV 101..89

Reflection 21- More Devastation...91

Reflection 22- Wedding Bliss...95

Reflection 23- The Cycle Repeats..101

Reflection 24- "Wait! I Got Your Back!"..................105

Reflection 25- Release, It's Not About You!................109

Reflection 26- A Voice for the Voiceless...........................115

Poem: "A Letter Cause You're Gone".......................121

Thank You...122

Sources...125

Connect with the Author..126

Standing on my Healing: From Tainted to Chosen

My Dedication

This writing is dedicated to T-my Ace, my Pea in a Pod, my Broheim

August 30, 1969-July 13, 2015

Standing on my Healing: From Tainted to Chosen

Standing on my Healing: From Tainted to Chosen

Introduction

October 12, 2010

I started writing my book in 2008 then stopped. It's 2010 and I am at it again… Finally, I will try to complete it without a long stretch of time going by. I had no idea it will be so difficult to gather words to express my life as an HIV-positive woman. You sit and think about everything that led up to the day you received the news and all of the emotions you felt from the past, present and future. Then you begin to write each word as your heart fills with excitement about how this book will end. We all have a story to tell and this is mine.

Me

As I sit alone I begin to feel sad

Then I think of all the happiness in my life and I begin to get glad

As a little girl, I was surrounded by love

Then darkness for many years which bought on many tears and has made me mad

Seems like I will never ever be happy when I think of all the bad that has happened in my life

Violence, defeat, hurt, anger, sadness and strife

I thought at one point that those things were all I would ever endure for the rest of my days. Hmmm how odd.

Standing on my Healing: From Tainted to Chosen

Standing on my Healing: From Tainted to Chosen

Reflection 1

Tee and Lee

I am originally from Philadelphia Pennsylvania, West Philly to be exact. I am the oldest girl of seven children, two from mom and dad's first marriage, three from mom's second marriage and two from dad's second marriage. My oldest brother and I from mom and dad's first marriage, have always been close coming up. He was always there for me and was so much fun growing up with. We played and laughed all the time, as the youngest he always let me do just about anything to him. There were even times I was playing and I hurt him physically but he would forgive me without hesitation and love me unconditionally. I may have been about three years old and as him and I played in the bedroom, out of the blue playfully I hit him with the tray to my wooden highchair! You may ask, "what in the world did you do that for?" I really have no idea; we always play so rough that I didn't think anything of it…that is until I saw the blood coming from his mouth. I had busted my brother's lip and it seemed like so much blood to me, boy was I scared. Any sibling would've took it to you and would have been angry but not my big brother. He told me it was okay even after I cried and said I was sorry. That scar on his upper lip stayed there the rest of his life. Then there was a time he was riding his bike up and down the street and I pushed him into sticky bushes! I know, I know it was mean, but I was only playing; we always played rough. The final episode with my big brother allowing me to do what I wanted was a night we were playing in the bedroom but he fell asleep before I did so while he slept I put my beads from a little purse in his ears. You remember the beaded purses little girls had with those very tiny beads on them? Yeah those, he still had some beads in his ear canal as an adult,

Standing on my Healing: From Tainted to Chosen

smh. Gosh I was mean in a playful way… how is that? At any rate my big brother loved me so much that he never got upset with me.

During this time, may be 1975 or 1976, my parents were divorced my big brother and I lived with mom. I remember always having big Christmases and birthdays. Mom showed us so much love. We saw our dad a lot which was a good thing. I remember when he came to pick us up he was sometimes on his bike. It was fun riding on dad's bike, I remember dad teaching me how to tie my shoes and grand pop teaching me how to clean ears of corn. Despite my parents not being together anymore I still felt so much love with the both of them, things were great! Mom eventually got into another relationship which I didn't mind because he always gave my big brother and I 50 cent pieces when he came around. Fifty cents meant a whole lot of candy and cookies and the 70s! My big bro and I always put our candy together which made it seem like we could open our own little candy store.

The sunshine in my little life began to dim when my big bro left us to go live with dad. After 30+ years I still remember that day clearly. We were all at my grandmother's house in West Philly because there was a birthday party there. For some reason my mom and dad were arguing and my brother was saying he wanted to go live with my dad. I wanted to be with them both so all I could do was cry. See as time went on my mom's new man started to get really mean to my brother and I. His disciplinary tactics were too extreme more so towards my brother which is why he wanted to go live with dad. Anyway, during the fight between my dad and mom I remember them fighting over me. Dad had one arm and mom had the other, they were playing

Standing on my Healing: From Tainted to Chosen

tug-of-war with me because they both wanted me with them. My brother wouldn't budge even after I asked him to stay with me, he was adamant about going with dad. During the tug-of-war session dad finally let go because I was crying that I wanted to stay with mom, plus they didn't want to hurt me. They both asked me what I wanted and I said that I wanted them both. I knew that wouldn't work so I chose mom. Dad hugged and kissed me then let me go. As I'm sitting here writing this book I remember it was devastating as a little girl to have your best friend leave… My big brother.

Well, after a little while we had visitations which allowed me to see my dad and my brother again. By this time my mom was remarried and had a set of twins who I didn't like because I didn't like their father. My dad was remarried also and I had a little brother and sister. I really like them especially my sister because I was only a few years older than her and we played a lot. During the visits my dad's new wife was very mean to me and my big brother but I never said a word because I didn't want the visits taken away. Sadly, to say the day I dreaded came where I could not see my brother anymore. My mom's new husband was very abusive and during a domestic violence episode he hit my brother with a dead bolt lock. My brother left to go back with dad and then bad headaches entered my life as well as nightmares. I would have a dream that my big bro and I would go to the penny candy store and on the way home he would slip and fall in the sewer and I would be crying holding him by his hand trying to pull him up then I would wake up. I would always wake up crying and then would have really bad headaches. My big bro and I would talk on the phone sometimes but it was not the same, I really missed him and needed him.

Standing on my Healing: From Tainted to Chosen

Standing on my Healing: From Tainted to Chosen

Reflection 2

Rocky's Double Trouble

When my twin sisters were born, I became my mom's little helper. They were a handful... DOUBLE TROUBLE! When one was hungry the other one was hungry so mom fed one and I fed the other. When one pooped the other pooped at the same time. I was happy to help mom because it brought us closer and allow me to step in my big sister role. My sister's father was very mean to my mom physically, verbally, mentally and emotionally. He didn't lay a hand on me but he always called me out of my name, he always called me an ugly black B&%$#. Mom combated the horrible things he said to me by saying the opposite to me than what he did. She was such a loving mommy despite being abused, she never mistreated us and we were well taken care of. Mom eventually got pregnant with my youngest sister but the abuse didn't stop, it got worse. I began to get closer to my twin sisters not just because I got used to them but I felt I had to protect them from their dad. His way of disciplining active pretty little girls was not right in my opinion. Even though I didn't like them when they were born I really love my sisters and wanted to make sure they were protected.

I tried to stay active in school and I had lots of friends. At home I was sure to be extra good so that when I asked mom if I could go outside she would say yes. Mommy worked really hard to take care of us, even though she was married he didn't really help. There was always a cost for mom if he did anything for her or the household. With mom working so much I had a lot of responsibility which meant growing up a little faster than I wanted to. Lots of chores, helping my sisters with homework, cooking, laundry, doing hair, bathing the girls, etc. Whatever mom needed I tried to help with.

October 29, 2010

As the twins got older I had to start taking them with me when I went to hang with my friends. I didn't like it at all but what older sibling would LOL. Even though I didn't want to take them with me, when I did, no one would mess with them or it was on! I had to protect them outside and no one better had even acted like they wanted to do something to them!

I started school in West Philly off of 52nd St. and I went to another school in Oak Lane for a brief time then some school in the North East; but my favorite was Henry Howard Houston Elementary School in Mt. Airy. I attended Houston from the second grade to the eighth grade, it was K through eight. In the beginning, it was rough because I was the new kid, I was shy and quiet plus so many people picked on me. In the second grade, I got chickenpox and when I returned to school the whole class said, "CHICKENPOX GIRL!" it was so embarrassing. I don't remember the third and fourth grades that well but I remember the fifth grade. That was the year that Marvin Gaye was killed by his father. It was very devastating worldwide. I come from a family of musicians and singers so I truly loved music and knew the artists. Just like most of us 70s babies. I also had my first little boyfriend in the fifth grade... He was so cute! I remember him getting crushed between two cars in the sixth grade. He survived but we were all so sad

Standing on my Healing: From Tainted to Chosen

because the accident stunted his growth and made him severely sick at times, but we stayed friends up until we were like 21 years old. I lost contact with him though.

I really remember a particular event in the seventh grade. I was good friends with one of my classmates and one Tuesday afternoon she comes to me with a crowd of girls saying that she was told I said she stinks. Even though she did stink I was definitely not the one who said it. She was my friend and I really thought she would have believed me when I told her I sincerely did not say it. Well, she tells me she wants to fight me Friday after school and its Tuesday. I remember the day well because school let out at 2:15 PM every Tuesday. Now at this point I had never had a fight a day in my life and I was scared! What made it so bad is it was Tuesday and she wanted to wait until Friday! The kicker of it all was when I had some of the roughneck girls tell me I better fight her and if I did not they would beat me up and if I did fight and win they would beat me up and if I lost they would beat me up. Okay how fair is that?! Talk about petrified, you have no idea. This started in the morning and by lunch I told her we were fighting that afternoon at 2:15pm when school let out. I felt tormented and I just couldn't go through that all week, I wanted to get it over with. That day it felt like time was at a standstill. So many things were going through my head like: "I have to pick up the twins after school, they are in kindergarten and I have to protect them, if I get beat up I'll get jumped, if I win I will get jumped, but worst of all if I got home and mom found out I got beat up or something happened to my sisters she was going to KILL ME!!" Kids can be so cruel.

Standing on my Healing: From Tainted to Chosen

October 31, 2010

    I was so afraid, I had never had a fight before and did not even know if I could fight. Then if we got caught fighting we would get suspended then mom was definitely going to take me out! No one really fought on school grounds so we all went behind the school over to the school for deaf children on some side street away from the school. As the day grew to an end I prepared for this fight I was dreading. The bell rang and I went to the kindergarten yard to pick up the twins. When I got to them I wanted to run out the front with them and disappear but I had people making sure that I got to this fight. I told the twins what was going on and also told them that if anything happened to me they were to run like crazy to an adult are back to the school. The twins and I hold hands and walked toward the back of the school with a crowd of students following. We get to the deaf school and I remind my sisters of what I said earlier and had them to sit by the gate away from the crowd. The girl I was going to fight had long nails and long hair so someone braided her hair to keep me from pulling it and even gave her Vaseline to put on her face! I was a serious nail biter so I had no nails and my hair was short. As we prepare for this fight, the other girls reminded me about what would happen to me if I won the fight or if I lost the fight. Someone had a metal pipe, someone else even had a homemade knife! Then it hit me, I had to literally fight for my life and keep my twins safe! The girl and I stood in the middle of the field and I began to look around and I noticed that almost the entire school was out there! I thought to myself, "man they are going to clown me in school!" People were yelling, "FIGHT, FIGHT, FIGHT"; then someone pushed me into her and I accidentally mushed her and she fell. I was just catching my balance with her face, it was truly unintentional. She then got up and called me a black B&^%$ which set off a spark in me. You see, my step dad always called me an ugly black B&^%$. It really bothered me especially with all of my siblings and my mom being light-

Standing on my Healing: From Tainted to Chosen

skinned and I was dark skinned. I had a color complex for real and low self-esteem. Mom used to always say "the blacker the berry the sweeter the juice". She always made me smile but inside I was still hurting. So, when the girl called me that name the next thing I know she was screaming, "MY EYE, MY EYE, MY EYE!" I had knocked her right in the face with my fist. While she was down I figured the fight was over so I went to go get my stuff and my sisters so we could leave but the girls who threatened me blocked me so I would not leave. The girl then came at me swinging her arms wildly and I weaved her windmill and punched her in the face. She covered her face while crying and by now I'm angry because these other people are threatening me, my little sisters are alone, and my stepdad was a hateful man, I had low self esteem, and I hated our home life. I felt so much rage and I began to take it out on her by beating her in her face with my fists… Literally. Somehow the girl grabs my arm and began to bite it. I'm trying to get her off of me but she is locked on my arm like a pit bull! I swing her around and we fall to the ground, while she is still biting my arm! My twin sisters come running to us and they started kicking her in her head. Once she lets go I am on top of her punching her in her face with both of my fist while I am enraged. I finally get off of her especially since she is no longer fighting back and I yell, "who is next? Who else wants some?!!" At least that's what I remember saying. Any fear I had was gone! No one stepped up or said anything even the ones who threatened me before. I took my sisters by the hand and began to walk home. One of my male classmates ran up to me and tied his belt around my arm tight saying the girl could have rabies and I didn't want to catch it, then he walked me home. I had a crush on him but never said anything of course so I felt really good that he walked me home and gave me his belt. When my sisters and I got home they busted in the door yelling, "Leesha was fighting, Leesha was fighting!!" My mother was on the phone at the time so she calmly hung up and said, "did you win?" Before I could answer my

Standing on my Healing: From Tainted to Chosen

sister said, "yes she beat the mess out of her! But she bit Leesha like a dog!" My mom looked at the bite and saw that the girl bit me through two shirts, a long sleeve shirt and a long-sleeved sweater!

November 22, 2011

My mom immediately took me to the doctors for a tetanus shot. I was so upset that I got bit but me winning the fight built my confidence. The next day at school everybody was talking about the fight and how I "tore her up". I never had so much attention from my classmates and it was great! Then I got the call I dreaded; a call to the principal's office. I was really nervous because I've never been in trouble or had to go to the "office". When I got there my mom was there, the girl I fought, her father and Mr. Davidson (rest in peace). You didn't want to get called to his office at all! I remember he used to give kids beatings and all I kept thinking was that I pray my mom doesn't allow him to beat me. Things turned out differently than I thought. The girl's dad was very upset because he said he had to put his dinner on her eyes to get the swelling down., his steak dinner. Mr. Davidson told me I should have walked away and I responded by asking him would he walk away if a man came up to him and hit him? He said I was out of line and should watch my mouth; in other words, that was a no! The decision was made that me and the girl both stay away from each other. That was hard because we had classes together, she used to be my friend. Before lunch the pain from the tetanus shot really kicked in and had me crying, that gave the girl I fought leverage to tell people I was crying because she beat me up. When I heard what she was going around saying I confronted her and dared her to say it to my face. The entire seventh grade was out there and of course she wouldn't say a word. I threatened to beat her even worse if I heard anything else from her. Needless to say, she never opened her mouth.

June 15, 2011

Wow, talk about feeling popular for the very first time! I didn't have problems out of anyone ever during the rest of my school days. I was also given the nickname "Rocky" by some of my fellow classmates LOL. One time in high school some girl stepped to me because I accidentally stepped on her foot. The people around me said to her, "you don't want to mess with Rocky!" The girl stepped off after that. Funny how things follow you.

Reflection 3

The Greatest Love of All

It is December 8, 2011 and I'm on my way to Philly with my dad and his wife. This is the weekend of his anniversary so we are giving him a surprise dinner but he thinks I'm taking him to a concert… Oh joy surprises! I haven't been in Philly since July 2011 when we had a reunion on my mom's side then my dad's side… The trips were interesting. I also haven't written in six months so I'm trying to write as much as I can this time.

July 7, 2011

This is a poem I wrote one day when I was feeling really down.

Will I ever love again?

That's the question I ask

it isn't because I don't think

I can it is because I don't know

if anyone would ever love me for who I am

I am beautiful I am talented

I have a beautiful smile

Standing on my Healing: From Tainted to Chosen

I can cook I can clean I can pray

but I am tainted. People are afraid

of people like me. I am liked I am loved

all as a friend, never a lover, or wife

in the end, I just pray for a better life...

I thank God I am healed set free and delivered

December 9, 2011

    Grade school was really not that bad, as a matter of fact it was very memorable and the most fun I had as a kid. Once I got in the 8th grade things got really bad at home between my mom and her husband and that violence. We were in and out of abuse shelters, going from place to place in hiding from the abuse and I missed a lot of school. We lived in a nice house in a nice neighborhood and looked the part but it was hell on wheels in the inside of the house. Mom did all she knew how to take care of us and show us love despite the circumstances. One would ask why didn't she just leave, well back then it was not easy especially with children. I remember when the time was getting close to 8th grade graduation and my science teacher told me that I was not going to graduate because I had not returned my text books. I was so heartbroken because I could not just go home and get the text books to return them. You see my mom's husband burned them along with some of our other items in the fire place during a domestic dispute between he and my mom. My mother contacted the school principal to explain why I could not return the books and he made the final decision that I would indeed graduate with my

Standing on my Healing: From Tainted to Chosen

class that year! I was so excited but there was still one problem, I didn't have anything to wear nor did I have shoes for graduation. During the months before graduation and the domestic dispute I would go to the mall and window shop for graduation dresses and there was this particular dress that I wanted which was $100 but I knew my mom could not afford to get it and shoes too plus get my hair done. I could not find any other dress that caught my eye so I kept looking in every store I could. A week before graduation I went back to the store where I saw the dress that I like just to look around again hoping I could find something nice yet inexpensive. When I walked in I went over to where the dress was which was still there and looked at the price tag hoping the price dropped and to my surprise it was marked down to $20.00!!! I could have screamed!! I grabbed the dress off the rack, tried it on again to admire myself in it then I paid for it and left the store with my head held high and a big smile on my face. My best friend at the time was with me and offered to let me borrow a pair of her shoes that went great with the dress and some jewelry. I loved to do hair and was pretty good at it so I did my own hair and my mother did my makeup. I was gorgeous, at least I felt that way even if it was for only one day. Our class song was Whitney Houston's version of The Greatest Love of All. I was so happy that day, happier than I have ever been in a long time.

Reflection 4

Making Adult Decisions

December 24, 2011

Today is a great day! I slept fairly well then I got up and had a nice 40-minute workout, got dressed and treated myself to an Indian Cuisine Buffett. The food is great, the atmosphere is relaxing and the décor is very nicely done. One of my dear friends in Philly took me to an Indian cuisine in the beginning of December and I made a vow to myself that id find one in Greensboro and treat myself to it…I am so glad that I did. It really feels great to be flaying her by myself with my thoughts. Sometimes that's what you need to relax, reflect and release. I'm not with family this year but it is ok they understand and I will see them soon. I really miss my mom and I love her dearly, I'll surprise her for Mother's Day though. Well, I'm going for my second plate now and I will continue writing a little later. Happy Holidays to me! P.S. Got my gift from my secret Santa and it was just what needed, a gorgeous watch! God is good!!

March 31, 2012

Yes, it has been 3 months since I wrote and some pretty awesome things have happened since then. I will eventually get to those things at some point in this book but in the meantime, I need to finish or continue where I left off.

Standing on my Healing: From Tainted to Chosen

High school was scary for me because nothing went the way that I planned for it to go. I wanted to go to the Philadelphia Performing Arts School to sing so I auditioned and sang Klymaxx's 'I Miss You'. I was so nervous but my big brother trained and helped me rehearse for a while, so even though I was nervous I was pretty sure that I was going to do well, he was such a great teacher. Even though my brother gave me the instrumental version to sang from I performed it acapella at the audition and still did great! The judges clapped and even stood up! I was so extremely happy because I knew I was going to be accepted now, they told me I did great! I waited a few weeks and finally received the letter in the mail from the performing arts school which started with, "Thank you for your interest in the Philadelphia School of the Performing Arts but unfortunately..." I was devastated! All I could do was cry. I passed the audition with flying colors but my school attendance was dreadful due to the constant moving from the domestic violence in our household. I even received a recommendation letter and received straight A's from the school I attend at the women against abuse shelter, but it wasn't enough. I ended up at Martin Luther King High School and you could not tell me that may world was not coming apart! Pulled from my very close friends and sent somewhere I dreaded going. All I could say to myself was that I could not do anything right, I was a failure.

Well, it was not that bad at King. I made new friends, I ran track and cross country, plus I sang in the school choir briefly. I got used to the school and told myself that I can do this. I was not the popular girl at all as a matter of fact I was very quiet and stayed to myself. My very best friend at the time since I was 12 years old lived in North Philly where I used to hang out a lot. She went on the prom with my big brother and they dated briefly. Her and I became so cool from the start. She liked the same things that I did, we both could sing, jump double Dutch, loved to

Standing on my Healing: From Tainted to Chosen

laugh and have fun together. I was even allowed to spend weekends at her house with her family where I got treated just like I was a part of their household. I did chores and got in trouble just like the rest of them. I sure did love that girl like she was my sister from birth. One day while visiting, one of her older male family members took interest in me and showed me some attention and as a rejected, quiet girl with low self-esteem and an adult shaped body I was glowing from the attention that he gave me. I was 13 years old when I met him and he would buy me candy, my favorite stuffed animals and even music albums or cassettes. I felt so loved, safe and accepted for the first time. You see, I was afraid of the opposite sex because of the things I saw not only in my home but almost everywhere during the 70's and 80's. Domestic violence. It was the norm in my world and as a very naïve teenage girl I thought that if you did not do what a man told you to do then he would beat you and I was not about to let that happen to me. With that being said, whatever this older male told me to do I did it whether I wanted to or not. Even down to sex. I was a 13-year-old virgin and he was a 19-year-old man. Even when I cried and told him that I didn't want to do it he told me I HAD to because he bought me things and if I loved him I would do it. There were times he would meet me after school then walk me to the park after getting me something eat or buying me other treats then make me perform sexual acts on him, sometimes until I vomited. I was too afraid to tell anyone not even my mom or my friends. There were times that I was really sick and I cried telling him 'no' but he insisted and I had to. One day while I was running in a cross country meet I was feeling so sick but I ran anyway and did very poorly. Another day while I was in class I was feeling so sick all I could do was cry and sit there, I couldn't get up or move my body. One of my male class mates picked me up and carried me to the nurse's office. Through my sickness, I was surprised that he helped because this guy always called me names and picked on me he even hit me sometimes but I

Standing on my Healing: From Tainted to Chosen

guess inside he did have compassion. I don't even remember the things the nurse asked me because it was so many years ago but I am sure she asked about my menstrual cycle and other feminine things but the next thing I know they were sending me home. My mother took me to the doctors to find out what was making me so sick and there I found out I had an upper respiratory infection and I was about 3 months pregnant! I am about to turn 14 years old, a good girl in school, I'm athletic, and a baby carrying a baby! What am I going to do??? My mom is going to kill me! My mother was so upset with me and it showed every single time she looked at me, boy did I walk on egg shells every time I came near her. I didn't know what to do, I was so afraid and all I wanted to do was ask my mom to hold me so that I could tell her what I was REALLY going through. She even told me that she knew I was pregnant because she could see it in my face and my body. My mom truly assumed that I was out there messing with guys, but never knew that I was terrified of men and didn't want them to come near me let alone touch me.

My mother had a friend at planned parenthood so we went for an appointment one day. There were people outside picketing with signs and yelling things and that made it even more scary. During my wait to be seen my mom didn't say a word to me, the anger she showed was evident to me how she felt. When I was called in the room I was allowed to go in by myself. The counselor was my mom's fiend so I felt a little comfortable but I just cried a lot. She explained to me a number of things as well as my options to keep the child, put it up for adoption or abort. I had no idea what decision to make, I am a child why do I have to make this decision!!! I just want to die!! I made a grown-up decision and opted for the abortion. I told the guy that got me pregnant that I need an operation which my family could not afford so he needed to give me $350.00 for it. He gladly gave me the money not even realizing what it was for. He said he was

Standing on my Healing: From Tainted to Chosen

coming with me but I told him he could not because my mother hated him and did not want him around, plus I did not want him to know that I was killing his child. See, there were times he would come around knocking on my door asking for me and my mom told him to never come around again because she knew he was too old for me. He would still sneak and come by when he thought she wasn't home so she felt like I told him to come but I never did. A few weeks went by before the appointment and by then I was at least 4 months and showing but I wore big clothes so no one actually knew what was going on. Then the day I dreaded came. The day of the abortion. When I got to planned parenthood, there were people still outside picketing and yelling obscenities about abortion so I had to come through the back door of the center. It was the scariest day of my life even more than when I almost drowned in a swimming pool at age 12. I told my mom that I was really scared then she said, 'oh so you want to keep it now????'. I said, 'no mom I'm just scared and I want you to hold my hand!'. I started to cry and she held my hand. We walked into the room which had all white walls and a single reclined type bed in it and a vacuum. I do not recall if I was given any form of relaxation drugs or pain killer intravenously but I remember the smell of rubbing alcohol which was like a hospital smell. My mom says that a salt saline fluid was inserted in me to relax the fetus growing in me to help make the process easier. This was not easy at all and I can only imagine for an innocent unborn child who had no idea what was about to happen. The vacuum was loud to me with a humming and sucking affect.

Tears ran down my eyes as they started the procedure but I wanted to see what was happening. My mom looked and she had such a terror on her face but she held my hand tighter then stood in my view so I could not see but only hear. The tube from the vacuum was clear so you could see parts of the fetus going through the tube. Yes, this is graphic! It was absolutely

Standing on my Healing: From Tainted to Chosen

terrible but I am writing this book this way so that you can live inside of my past life to really know who I am and the things that I endured, through God's grace despite decisions that I made. I'm a 14 yr. old 9th grader who had sex, got pregnant and had an abortion. I am like so many other girls. I had to stay strong because I refused to let people know what really happened to me and what I did while I was out of school, I just told people I was sick with an upper respiratory infection from a cold which was partially true. I never felt the same after that dreadful day.

Eventually the father of the baby I was carrying found out what I did after I stopped speaking to him and rejected his calls, he then inquired why from my best friend at the time. I eventually talked to him and he cried saying that I should have told him because he wanted the baby. I was angry and told him that I WAS A BABY!! I refuse to be with anyone who forced me to do things that I did not want to do. That abortion decision gave me the strength to stand up for me.

Reflection 5

I Adored Him

I attempted to go back to living my life as a normal teenaged girl, whatever that meant. The relationship with mom and I was strained because I did not talk, she was stressed and never knew the real reason things went the way they went for me. I hung out with friends and still did what I was supposed to in school and around the house but every chance I got to be outside that is where I was. One day I met a guy who was so fun and cool and he loved the singing group New Edition just as much as I did if not more. He knew every song, had every album like I did, and even knew most of their dance routines. He gave me the nickname 'Angel' and I gave him the nickname 'Snuggles' because he always snuggled with me. He was my little high school sweetie (smile) and you could not tell us we were not in love. Well, that didn't last very long because he ended up moving and going to another school but we stayed in touch as well as continued to stay friends for years even though we had new people in our lives. By the time I turned fifteen I found out what love at first sight meant. I was in North Philly at my best friend's house like normal, man I loved that girl to pieces!! She was my 'sister girl'. Anyway, we were in her bedroom blasting music and singing like mew always did plus making up dance steps. After a while we decided to go downstairs and while coming from the third floor where her room was we were giggling and laughing in the dark and once we made it to the second floor we bumped into someone. BOOM!! We both screamed like the girls we were because no one was in the house but her and I at the time. She turned on the lights and screamed again calling the person's

Standing on my Healing: From Tainted to Chosen

name and hugging him while I stood there with my mouth opened. In my eyes, he was so fine! Not just his looks but how he was dressed and carried himself was a total attraction. Silk shirt, dress pants, clean haircut, nice shoes. Mmmm mmmm hmmm, I was turned on just like that! Then he spoke to me introducing himself to me as we made eye contact, I said to myself, "whoa and a gentleman too! I have got to get his digits!" My shy nervous tail wouldn't dare ask thought (lol). When it was time for me to go home he offered to walk me all the way to the sub (train station for you non-Philadelphians) which was about 8 blocks. As we walked we ask questions about one another and once we got to the station he waited with me until my train came and got on the train with me since he was going the same direction. When his stop came, he stayed on the train with me for the next three stops after his to make sure I got off safely. I thought we were going to say goodbye but low and behold he got off with me and said he wanted to be sure I got on my next bus! Ok I was so through - this dude is a catch! He was so nice he did not ask for my number or push up on me at all which was so different for me. When I got home I called my bestie to let her know I got home safely and to tell her to give him my phone number. Then she said he told her to give me his number, man I was so excited, but that chick teased me and waited two days to give it to me and to give him my number! I could have gone through the phone after her for making us wait like that. Needless to say, he called me, asked me on a date to the movies and I definitely said yes without hesitation. My mother was not pleased to hear about this date especially since I had the abortion a year before this and to top it off the guy I got pregnant by was my best friend's uncle and this new guy was her brother. My best friend and the new guy had a different mother and father but her siblings and her had the same mom and her siblings had the same dad as the guy I just met. So technically they were step brother and sister but we didn't say that back then we just said simply that's my brother or that's my sister. As far as my mother

Standing on my Healing: From Tainted to Chosen

was concerned they were still family and she did not approve. Since our relationship as mother and daughter was shaky I really didn't care what she thought I was still going out with him.

    I got ready for our first date that day which we were supposed to meet downtown for the movies but his paycheck got stolen so we were not able to go. He was very upset and even embarrassed to tell me but I told him it was ok and we did not have to spend money we could just go somewhere and talk. See I was not used to a guy asking me out let alone being really nice and respectful to me so going out or not going out did not phase me one bit. He met me at the train station when I got to North Philly and walked with me to his house where he lived with his grandmother. I was really nervous going there because I lived in Mt. Airy and he lived in the heart of North Philly so it was basically a suburban quiet girl being with the open and friendly 'bad boy' but he was not a bad boy at all. He was extremely smart, in school, he worked, he was respectful and he was so clean cut. Anyway, we got to his house where he introduced me to his family and we watched television for the entire time I was there. He did not try to touch on me, kiss me or do anything inappropriate; he was a perfect gentleman and then walked me back to the subway, got on it with me and watched me as I got on the bus to go home. I called him when I got home and we stayed on the phone until one of us fell asleep. I was in heaven. We did as much as we could together when we could like park walks, the movies, walking downtown and video arcades. We had so much fun and he never made a sexual move on me. We were both in school and had jobs but we made time for one another. He had his own home demons he was dealing just like I did but we escaped them by spending time together - we were perfect. I remember the first day he asked me if it was alright to kiss me and I was very nervous but I said yes. We had been seeing each other for six months without touching or messing around which was a long time for young people when I was coming up. We stood there kissing for so long while I was leaning on the edge of the television that when we stopped kissing my legs were stiff and I was unable to move around without assistance. I loved that dude so much that I would have done anything for him, within reason that is. About three months later, when I was sixteen years old, we made decision to go all the way. Knowing all that I had been through before allowing him into my heart he asked me before even attempting to do anything with me. The fact that he was so affectionate and loving toward me brought me to tears. Our favorite song was 'Adore' by Prince. I was truly in love and no one could tell me differently, not because of anything physical but because I truly felt like someone finally loved me for me.

Eventually my mother was in a new relationship and I did not get along with her new mate so I spent all of my time away from home. I went to school in the morning, then straight to work and later on to visit my boyfriend for a few hours. We were truly inseparable. Things began to get so bad at home between my mother's man and I that one day I heard them arguing over his desire for me to leave. At age seventeen I left home, my mom's man did not like me and I did not like him. Feeling more rejection, I left home and went to my boyfriend's house crying. He had his own place by now and welcomed me with open arms. I cried for like two days about leaving home and refused to go to school, work or back home. He put his foot down one day and had a conversation with me about getting may tail back to school and work. I loved him and he was absolutely correct so I went to school and work even though I was depressed. He always pushed me to do the right thing and never agreed with me not going to school, I felt safe with him but I missed my mother.

Reflection 6

Young, In Love, and Blind

It is December 1989, my boo and I are celebrating his birthday and enjoying our time together. Out of the blue he says to me, "Let's make a baby!" and I was all for it! Now I knew we did not have a lot of money and the place we lived in was too small and definitely not suitable for a baby but I knew that with us both working we would eventually get a bigger and better place. I was happy about it despite all of the negative things that were surrounding me because now I will have someone to love unconditionally and who will love me back, my baby. My boo's birthday was December 1 which was the last time I had my menstrual cycle. Now before we made the decision to have a child together there were a few things going on that was suspicious such as money missing periodically so I decided to ask what was going on. My boo explained to me that he owed money to a drug dealer before he met me and was trying to pay the guy back but did not have enough money. I asked what he owed and told him that I would help him so he told me that it was $100.00. I told him that it was no problem and I would get the money for him. I had been saving money for us so that we could move and I knew I was about to get a little more so I gave him the $100.00 out of love for him and honesty, fear of the one he owed money too. After giving him the money what I had been saving still kept coming up short; this had me bewildered because my boo knew that we were trying to move to a better place. Well, one day I came home from work and the landlord asked me for the rent money. I told him he needed to talk to my man because he paid him but the guy insisted that he was not paid. I was

Standing on my Healing: From Tainted to Chosen

dreadfully afraid of this man because we would hear him beat his wife up constantly, so I told him he had to wait and I quickly went upstairs to my room.

I was all too familiar with domestic violence having grown up in a household full of it and be surrounded by it for the majority of my life so I knew to stay clear of him. I went upstairs to my room but remained afraid because more than anything I did not want my landlord coming upstairs to ask me more questions or to take his demands for money to an all-time high. I could not wait for my boyfriend to get home - where was he? I checked the area where I put the money I was saving so that I could double check how much we had because I wanted to leave as soon as possible before that landlord decided to flip his lid on us. Wait a minute!! Where is all of my money? The money I had saved was gone right down to the last penny. There were no cell phones, we did not have a house phone or a pager and I had no idea where my boyfriend was so all I could do was wait. A little while later my boyfriend came in as I was sitting on the edge of the bed playing a video game and trying everything I could to hold my composure. He looked really antsy, strange almost nervous so before jumping to conclusions I told him about the encounter with the landlord. He then told me to stay upstairs and he would go speak with him. I was not a combative girlfriend so I did what he said but I listened in the hallway. The men exchanged some words and I overheard the landlord tell my boyfriend that we had to leave tonight if he did not have the rent we owed for three months. THREE MONTHS? You have got to be kidding me! This news had me in complete shock because I had been giving my boyfriend my portion of the rent every month on time. He came upstairs and told me that the landlord wanted us to leave. I ask him about the money I had saved, and with his head down, he said he had to use it for something! This answer fueled an argument even more being that he would not provide any additional details about what had been going on all of this time. DRUGS? I knew he smoked weed but he could not be smoking so much weed that he would exhaust all of our funds including our savings. Boy was I naïve; I knew that it was more to this story yet there I was stuck with a man who had nothing and whose actions were about to cause us to be homeless.

When you are young and in love, your blindness can block the significance of what is going on around you. Some of us have grown up with low self-esteem issues, rejection, and a lack of identity so we search for love in all the wrong places or we just simply get caught up. I was so angry and sad but most of all I was scared. I could not go back with my mom nor did I want to; my boyfriend and I had nowhere to go and it was late so finding a place that night was not an option. We went downtown for a reason I cannot remember, possibly to sleep in the park on a bench. He reassured me that everything would be alright and he told me to lay on his lap and as I began to fall asleep it started raining. We got up and went to the subway where there is shelter but nowhere to sit except on the steps. We sat on the steps and without talking he motions me to lay back on his lap so I can sleep and covers me with newspaper as I lay shivering, cold and damp. Oh, did I mention that I was pregnant? Yeah, possibly a few weeks by now.

Despite all of the negative events surrounding me I was really happy that I was pregnant. Now I have someone to love unconditionally and who will love me back, my baby! I really had a rough pregnancy, not only did I deal with morning sickness but I had other complications which placed me in a 'high risky pregnancy' status category. In the midst of the homelessness, there were times when I would go days without eating because I was not working and everything we did get went to fund my boyfriend's addiction. I spent many days in depression, rejection and missing my family; I just stayed very sick. I kept going to school as much as I could but the last month and a half before school was out I was too sick to attend resulting in me missing my high school graduation. Once again, I felt like I could not even do that right.

Standing on my Healing: From Tainted to Chosen

Reflection 7

What a Wonderful Life, Right?

High school was really a blur for me anyway but what I do remember from my senior year is being out for a while and when I came back I had no hair. It was so short I could not even roll it up with rice! You see, one day I realized that my hair was thinning very badly in the center so I decided to get braids hoping that my hair would grow from them. When it was time to take the braids out not only did the braids come out but so did my hair with them. The doctor said it was just stress and part of the hormone changes I was experiencing from the pregnancy. Talk about being at my lowest! The homeless situation grew worse and worse, eventually leading me back to my mom's through her invitation; I did not want to because of her man but my tiredness with being homeless and hungry far outweighed any of my dislikes. I truly needed a comfortable bed and a safer place to stay. My mom offered to give me a wig to wear to school but my response was," A wig! What am I going to hold it down with I am practically bald!" She told me I could use bobby pins but declined for fear of the wig still falling off. Off to school I went preparing myself for the massive teasing I would get from not just being pregnant but being bald too. I went to school and made it to my first class early before my classmates and sat down. I sat in the front of the class and kept my head kind of low so people would not recognize me. Once the class filled up and the teacher called roll I was so scared. After she finished someone said, "Diggs?" I turned around with my heart racing because the class got really quiet. I turned around and waved. I do not remember who the person was I only know it was a female then she

Standing on my Healing: From Tainted to Chosen

said, "Oh my gosh!! How are you? Where have you been? You look great!" In shock I replied, "I've been sick but I am getting better." She then said, "You're pregnant? Congratulations!" The class was still quiet even the teacher- the perfect atmosphere to feel shameful. She then said, "I love your hair cut, what made you do that?" At this point I was really feeling weird but not shocked by her comment. I replied, "I didn't cut it my hair fell out due to stress." After that everyone agreed that they thought it looked good on me and they liked it and missed me. Me? Who misses Alicia or even cares about her? I was so surprised at the positive responses from my classmates, that it made me feel better about myself for a little while. During my time back in school they all were planning for the senior prom and a trip to the Poconos. Many asked me to go on the trip with them but I declined due to pregnancy embarrassment. I was the only one pregnant and surely I was not going in this state or wear a bathing suit when everyone went swimming. As for the prom, my boyfriend said he would get himself together and his grandmother said she would help me get everything I needed if I would just stay in school. At the last minute, he decided that he was not going to go and of course there was not anyone else I could go with, so I did not go either; instead I sat home crying. I missed the prom, the senior trip and even graduation. Once again, I felt like I could not even do that right.

Mom got me a job at a video store she was the manager of so that I could have a little money in my pocket and save for the things my child needed when she was born. Yes, she! I prayed for a girl and was so happy when I found out I was having one. I used to say I did not want any children but if I ever had any I would only have two, a girl first then a boy. I enjoyed working there and actually did a great job at it. I was really starting to feel really happy and better about myself. I was back in school and had moved back with my mom; that happy feeling went away quick though. One day while working with my mom her boyfriend came to the job to visit her and for reasons I do not remember he and I got into an argument. Man, he was so hateful to me and we could not stand one another! He told me I was a lesbian; my boyfriend was a crack head and as a result my child was going to be a lesbian and a drug addict. The argument got so bad that he wanted me out of the house yet again. I eventually left and went back with my boyfriend to stay in a room he rented that had no running water or bathroom facilities. Oh what a wonderful life!

Standing on my Healing: From Tainted to Chosen

Reflection 8

Hungry, Sick and Tired

As an eighteen year old soon to be single mother I did not know what to do or where to go except back to the situation I was in. Many wanted to know why I did not go with other family but between being disconnected from my relatives and embarrassment over my situation in my eyes I was stuck. I eventually got on welfare and started receiving WIC (a food subsidy for Women, Infants and Children) and food stamps. Without proper living arrangements I could not go shopping to store food so I bought food every day to eat. There were even times that I sold stamps for money and sadly gave my boyfriend money when he would lie and tell me it was for something legit. Yes, in the back of my mind I knew he was still getting high but I was too weak minded to tell him no, plus the arguments between us were getting really bad and I was too sick and huge from my pregnancy to fight with him anymore. To top it off, I actually still loved him and believed that he would get himself together especially after our child was born. Sometimes you can be so caught up in a situation and so depressed with low self-esteem that you do not even know how to fight for yourself let alone reach out to people. To make matters worse I still loved the person who hurt me with all of my heart. Some people saw some of the things that were going on but no one really got in your business; in my opinion they had their own junk to deal with and really did not want another burden. I remember August 29, 1990 - I got up early because I had to go to the bathroom really bad so I walked from 13th and Lehigh to 17th and Lehigh in Philly where I lived at the time when I was a little over eight months pregnant. My

Standing on my Healing: From Tainted to Chosen

boyfriend had already left out earlier that morning so I got up and went to his best friend's house. His friend's mom would let me bathe, use the bathroom or feed me at times. My stomach was hurting but I assumed that I had to go to the bathroom. I arrived at her house, used the bathroom and washed off. She asked how I was and I told her I was alright then I left. I always felt embarrassed around everyone because here I was carrying a baby, practically homeless and with a drug addict boyfriend. I went outside and sat on the steps. I was out there for a few hours just sitting there. I did not want to walk too much because my stomach hurt and I did not want to aggravate it anymore with too much movement. After a few hours one of the girls on the block came outside and spoke to me and I spoke back. She then asked me a dreaded question; she said, 'Lee did you eat?" I said, "Yeah I ate not too long ago." She said," You lyin' you been sittin' here on the steps all morning and now it is the afternoon and I ain't see you eat nothin', come in here and get something to eat." I told her I was alright but she insisted and was getting irritated with me so I went in her house. He children's father, my boyfriend and a few other guys were in the back yard smoking weed and drinking beers. She and I sat in the kitchen and she made me Spaghettios (yeah I remember exactly what I ate because the after effects of the meal was unforgettable.) As I was sitting there eating her boyfriend came in and spoke to me then he asked her in an angry voice, "Why she eating our kid's food??" Oh boy my heart started racing. "Cause she hungry, she been sitting out on those steps all day and ain't eat!" His response was, "so why her man ain't feed her then?" Before I could say anything she replied saying, "Cause that nigga out there smoking and drinking like he always do and not feedin' his girl!" I told them I was about to go and I was sorry. Her man then said," Naw it ain't your fault and you ain't going nowhere!" He then addressed my boyfriend who was still having the time of his life saying, "Yo homey why you sitting out here smoking and drinking wit' us and your baby mom ain't eat

Standing on my Healing: From Tainted to Chosen

nothin'?? Nigga you ain'$%^&! That's wrong!!" Why did I come in this house? We are going to argue and fight for sure after this! The rest of the guys started doggin' my boyfriend out so as he was leaving he gave me a dirty look and told me to come on. The guy and his girl said, "No she ain't going nowhere with you so you can push her around and argue with her she eight months pregnant! You get out!" He left and I sat there for a few minutes then said I was leaving but his best friend told me to go to his house with his mom and not go home until things died down. I went up the street to his house, sat on the couch and fell asleep for a little while. When I woke up it was dark outside, I had a headache and my stomach was hurting so bad. I decided to leave because I needed to lay down. I walked back to 13th and Lehigh then got in the bed. I was sleeping when I heard him come in and slam the door. "Lee, you talk too %^&^ing much! Why you always running your mouth?" He started throwing my clothes out of the window and telling me to get out. I tried picking the clothes up and telling him to just leave me alone. He just kept on cussing at me and shoving me as I struggled to bend over to pick up the clothes. The next thing I know I was light headed, I slid down the wall outside and it got dark. When I woke up I was in the bed and honestly I do not even remember what he said to me besides the fact that he was sorry. As I came to myself, with my stomach hurting even more, I began wondering how I would ever get out of the situation before my baby came and this thought was the one that rocked me back to sleep.

Standing on my Healing: From Tainted to Chosen

Standing on my Healing: From Tainted to Chosen

Reflection 9

I'm Not Ready!

Between the stress of homelessness, having days of not eating due to lack of money, rejection, depression, and missing my family I stayed very sick. This was just not the life I thought I would be living, but hey it could be worse right? I remember waking up feeling really wet, I figured I wet the bed but when I checked, the wetness just did not seem like urine. I began to get really scared and decided I need to go get cleaned up. I put on a pair of white underwear since I did not have any sanitary napkins then I took the walk back to 17th and Lehigh. Man that was a really painful and tiring walk but I made it. I asked my boyfriend's friend's mom if I could use her bathroom. When I checked my underwear they were very wet and pink inside. I found myself scared out of my mind knowing that I was not ready to even think about having my baby! After a little clean up and using tissue as a sanitary napkin I went outside and sat on the steps as usual. This day I did eat (I guess I had money or food stamps to get something to eat; things are so cloudy I just do not remember that far back.) As the day went on, extremely slow might I add, I noticed some of the other women around me looking at their watches every time I made a face or a sound. My stomach was hurting pretty bad but I played it off. They asked me if I was alright and of course I said I was but they gave me a look and said, "alright Lee". Later that evening I remember my boyfriend's grandmother making homemade hamburgers you know the ones with onions, and bell peppers from scratch not those frozen burgers and homemade French fries and man I was ready to eat. She asked me if I wanted a burger I told her I did. As the time of food preparation commenced it seemed as if the pain was at an all-time high! Next thing I know an ambulance comes down the street and I am thinking they are coming for the older lady on the block because they stopped right in front of us. The paramedics get out and say to me, "Ma'am you are in labor?" I said NO! Like everyone else had rehearsed it they said in sync, " Yes she is!" The paramedics helped me to my feet and I had another contraction. They asked how many minutes apart and I guess everyone said like 5-7 minutes apart. I told them I needed to get my burger but they kindly let me know that I was going to the hospital and will not be getting a burger at that point.

It is August 30, 1990 and my big brother Tj was celebrating his birthday. He told me he would come to the hospital with me but I told him to finish celebrating that I would alright. Besides, that boy was tore up!! I called my mom and told her I was in labor at the hospital, I was scared and wanted her there. She told me she was cooking spaghetti (my favorite) and when she was done she would come to the hospital. I remember it was after 7pm because the Cosby show was on at the time. The nurses had me walking the halls to induce labor but I was in so much pain that all I could do was scream and cry. My boyfriend was there but I really did not want him to be. I was disgusted at him for being a drug addict, for being so mean to me and for being so dirty. I wanted my mom. My doctor came and told the nurses I needed to be in the bed. They laid me down hooked me to monitors and insisted that I should breath, not yell and not to push yet. I asked them for water or ice chips but they would not budge. I told one of the nurses that I was really scared and to hold my hand as I tried to breath. I took a deep breath and for some reason could not let it out. I begin to black out. I could faintly hear them say, "her heart rate is dropping! Miss Diggs wake up! Wake up Miss Diggs!" Next thing I knew it was time to push.

Standing on my Healing: From Tainted to Chosen

At 7:03am on August 31,1990 I gave birth to a 6lb 13oz beautiful baby girl who I named Charisma Denise Wilson Diggs and we all called her Riz or Rizzy. I named her after my youngest sister's middle name because I thought it was so beautiful. When my sister was born in 1983 I said when I had my first daughter I would name her Charisma, and I did just that. I was happier than I had ever been in my entire life that all I could do was cry, stare in her pretty face and look at her big pretty eyes. The doctor asked me why I kept crying and if it was because of my pain but even in that moment they could not understand the pure joy I felt of the miracle that rested in my arms. August 31, 1990 was a joyous day for me. The next day a social worker came in to discuss my living conditions and informed me that I would not be able to take my baby home with me until I had a safe place to take her. Remember, the place I lived in had no running water or bathroom facilities - it was a slum. How can I be a good mother bringing an innocent child in these disgraceful conditions? They told me they would give me a few hours but if I did not have a place to take her then they would put her in custody until I did. I was terrified!! What was I going to do? I had nowhere to go, I was an 18-year-old new mom, penniless, unmarried, incomplete education, and homeless with no family contact at the time.

I called my mother since I had no choice and no one else to call. I beat around the bush a little with her and then asked why she did not come to the hospital and she told me she got busy. I then told her what social services said and asked if I could come there with her until I got on my feet. Well, that did not work out so I was back to the beginning. Do not get me wrong, my mom loves me and I am sure she had her reasons during that time. I am not bashing my mom by any means but only stating what happened in my life in a way that is not hurtful to others but was real to me. After hanging up with my mom I held my baby tight not wanting to let her go and

Standing on my Healing: From Tainted to Chosen

still not knowing what I was going to do. I looked at the clock realizing that I had less than 15 minutes before Social Services would be back to take my baby from me. Then the phone rang. When I answered it the voice on the other line said in sternly, "Lee come home!" I said, "What do you mean come home?" She said, "You know what I mean, you and your baby come here until you get on your feet." I started crying and saying thank you. The voice was my baby's great grandmother, her dad's grandmother. She told me to stop crying and come on. Just then Social Services came in asking if I had a place to go and I gave them the address and whatever else they needed. I was able to keep my baby!! I called a cab and went to her great grandmother's house, my baby and I.

Riz's great grandmother had a baby shower for me and there were so many gifts for my baby that I did not have to buy anything for her for at least a year. I was so grateful to her more than words could express but it seemed that nothing I did or said was good enough to repay her for allowing us to stay and for the great gifts she provided. Gosh that woman was so dag on mean! Needless to say, I did not stay with her very long since my daughter's father got himself together well enough to get a place for all three of us. He got us a one bedroom studio apartment in my old hang out area on 52nd Street in West Philly. I felt like we could now be a family and things would be so much better.

Reflection 10

Just Tired

Jeremiah 29:11

For I know the thoughts I have toward you, says the Lord, thoughts of peace and not of evil, to give you a future and a hope.

After a little while I was able to get my diploma but then the family we had tried to re-create began to crumble. As I tried to be a good mom and girlfriend he was stepping out on me as he was so used to doing. I did not deserve it and neither did my daughter so as things went from bad to worse I contacted my mom and asked her if my child and I could stay with her and this time she agreed without hesitation. Once back with mom my focus was taking care of my baby and getting myself together so that she can have a stable lifestyle. I enrolled in barber school which was a huge dream for me. While I went to school my mom had my daughter and taught her colors, shapes and even potty trained her. I finally felt like I was doing a little something right for a change. Yes, I would still see my daughter's father off and on because I still loved him and I did not want my daughter to not have her dad in her life. He and I never worked out; we were arguing and fighting over everything from money, him being in the streets all the time doing his thing, me badgering him to be a father to his child and a man in my life or we just plain did not get along. I was learning the hard way that a woman cannot make a man be what and who SHE wants him to be. She cannot expect him to take care of responsibilities or love the way she thinks he should when he never had anyone to show him let along give it to him. I was back and forth with my daughter's father and when I would go back to my mom's her man and I would be at each other's neck. In my mind it was HELL ON WHEELS! The dreams and desires I had dissolved right in front of me while I thought that I was doing the right thing in life; I truly thought I was loving right and parenting right. You see, there are no manuals out there for any of that. Everyone has their own opinion on how a person should live their life, love and even parent but everyone's opinion is different. 99.9% of the time we all just learn from experiences whether good or bad.

I was always looking for approval from someone or the answers to decisions in my own life. Some information was good, some was hard to hear, some was just plain wrong. With all that was going on in my so-called life I ended up being frustrated, angry, sad, lonely, depressed and even suicidal. I did not know then that the best manual for Alicia was the Word of God-JESUS! I remember when I was twelve years old and figured that if I died, my mom would not have to be subjected to the abuse that she endured, so I took 2 pills from a medicine bottle in the bathroom cabinet. Once I swallowed them I realized that I did not want to die but I could not bring the pills back up! I started crying saying, "Lord I do not want to die, I'm sorry!" If you let me live, I will be a good girl I will not do it again!". I laid on the bathroom floor and cried myself to sleep praying that I did not die that day. When I woke up it was so cold that I thought for a second that I was dead until I realized that I was on the bathroom floor. Boy was I happy!

How many know that when you plead with God that you will never do something again, most of the time you never even realize that you did not mean it until you do it again. My next suicide attempt happened when I was nineteen years old. I was arguing with my daughter's dad, not getting along with my mom, struggling severely yet again, trying to finish Barbering School and trying to be a mother. I was broken and I was seriously at my breaking point. One day during an argument outside with my daughter's dad I just could not take any more. I just got quiet and told him to take the baby because I was done. She was in her stroller and after getting him to take the stroller handle, I proceeded to walk in front of the city bus that was coming down the street. He pulled me back yelling, "Lee what is wrong with you?!!". I did not respond I just sat on the steps of someone's house where we were at the time, picked up a piece of glass and tried cutting my wrist. He smacked the glass out of my hand but I kept trying to get more glass to cut my wrist. The entire time I did not say a word, I felt like I was out of my body as if I was literally losing my mind. As much as I tried to cut myself pressing as hard as I could, the glass would not go through. In my mind, it was another failed attempt to do something I thought was right or the solution to the many problems I was dealing with. The next morning I was still very sad, still alive and could not even kill myself right. My daughter's father and I eventually broke up and I went to live with my mother, again. During that time, I had no idea that God had a plan for my life, I did not even know God I just knew of Him.

Standing on my Healing: From Tainted to Chosen

Reflection 11

The Older Man

I was finally doing something in my life that I had been wanting since I was a little girl and things were finally looking up. While in barber school I gained my confidence back and I knew I would succeed. One day my mom and her man introduced me to his Puerto Rican friend whom I had no attraction to at all but my mother felt that he would be a good fit for me because he was older and financially stable. This man would not stay out of my face despite how I rejected him and even regardless to the age difference, he was 32 and I was 21. I eventually went out on a date with him and before I knew it my mother was insisting that it would be a good idea for me to move in with him so he can take care of me and my child since I clearly did not have money to take care of us on my own. Again, I had no attraction to this man whatsoever and only went out with him so he would leave me alone. He spent lots of money on me when we went out but that did not impress me at all. In my eyes, he was nothing more than an old man with money and a misfit when it came to the type of man I was attracted to. As the weeks went by he came around almost every day and before I knew it my mother was pushing me off again to live with him which added to the feelings of rejection. The guy pressed, my mother pushed, her man nagged and I eventually gave in. Here we go again making decisions based on what other people wanted and not what I wanted. Yeah, he had his own house and cars but I did not like this man and none of that mattered. So, my only motivation to go with him was the rejection I endured. I did not think my mom wanted me around and I definitely knew her man could not stand the thought of my being around so I left. Rejection is a terrible feeling because it causes you to feel

Standing on my Healing: From Tainted to Chosen

unloved, unwanted, depressed and unworthy causing you to make decisions that you know are not healthy just to feel accepted.

I tried to make the best of the living arrangements for my daughter and I that I felt so forced into. I never had to cook or go grocery shopping and anything I wanted, all I had to do was ask for it. We ate out for breakfast, lunch and dinner, plus he took me to barber school every single day and picked me up. I had it going on right? Heck NO!!! We ate out every day because he did not ALLOW me to shop or cook and insisted we go out or order in whenever we were hungry. He picked me up and took me home every day from school to prevent me from being with my friends and family. You are probably saying that you would not have put up with that and he would not have made you do anything that you did not want to do because you would…right? Yeah, well everyone says that when they are not in the same situation. Here I am the rejected, depressed, unloved single parent with no job, no self-esteem and nowhere else to go; yeah I did all of that if he said so. Besides, I was living in his house rent free and disconnected from my friends and my family. This man kept a gun in almost every part of the house. He had a gun under his pillow, under the mattress, under the bed, in almost every drawer and even in the car. If anyone, even the delivery guy, knocked on the door he would pick up a gun. Was he paranoid? I guess he was, even though he did not give off a crazy look or disposition. People on the outside saw him as the nicest guy there was. I guess it was the norm in his life to have guns all the time for everything. I hated guns. Since I could not spend any money I had or the food stamps I was getting I saved them so that I could move my daughter and I out of there the first chance I could. I just wanted to get as far away from him as quick as I could. That man was so dominant and silently crazy that one day I came home from school and he had

Standing on my Healing: From Tainted to Chosen

magazines and books all over the bed with pictures of the wedding ring I was to wear, the wedding dress, where we were getting married and what country we were going to live in! He even told me that I was going to have his son when I finally did have sex with him. (No I was not intimate with him because I did not like him and he never wanted to use a condom.) I told him that I would never marry him or have his child to which he replied with his resume' of women who only really wanted to be friends and would seek abortions in response to the news of being pregnant by him. I am saying to myself, "what the %&*^ did I get myself into!? I have got to find a way to get out of here!" I did not tell my friends about what I was going through because so many thought he was nice and I was embarrassed. I did tell a couple of my friends but they could not help me out of my situation. One day I confessed to one of my classmates because she saw me crying and she said she would keep an eye out for places and help me move when it was time.

I cannot believe that my life is always so screwed up! Was I created to be this way? It sure felt like it. One day he kept pressuring me about having intercourse with him because I had been there about a month and did not allow him to touch me. He just knew I was having relations with someone else but I told him it was impossible since he did not let me be with my friends or go anywhere by myself. I got so tired of his complaining and nagging about me not being intimate with him that I gave in one day. I insisted that he use protection but he refused to and told me I was going to have his son. I always gave in to certain situations when pressure was on me and I felt like it was no way out. I hated that part of me it was so weak and I always got caught up in some sort of bad situation because of being that way. That night after less than 5 minutes I knew I was pregnant. I knew I could not determine pregnancy after 5 minutes of unprotected sex but that night knew I was pregnant. The next day in school I confided in my classmate and told her about that night before but she started to laugh until she saw the tears filling in my eyes. She realized how truly unhappy I was in my situation. I absolutely did not want to be with this man let alone have his child; it felt like my life was ending. A little over a month goes by and I was in pain, feverish and just sick. When I went to the doctors they told me that I had fibroid tumors that needed to be removed. I scheduled an appointment for pre-op surgery which would take place in a few weeks but during the days leading up to the procedure, I began to feel worse. I knew I was pregnant because the sickness was so intense, morning sickness times 5! The day of pre-op of course he went with me and I did not want him to because if I was pregnant, which I knew I was, I did not want him to know. Even though I had an abortion at age 14, I found myself now at 21 years old, not agreeing with it but not wanting to have his child either. What in the world was I going to do? My life was full of hard decisions that I had to come to grips with and make a choice. I really just wanted to disappear.

As I walk in the room he wanted to come in but I said no. The nurse came in and started to explain things to me but I told her I thought I needed a pregnancy test first. She asks when my last period was and I guess I told her it had been past due for a few weeks or so but I knew I was pregnant. She gave me the test and I sit in the room waiting. As I sat there alone so many thoughts began running through my head like how I will hurt myself by falling down the steps or another method outside of an abortion because to kill this baby was not right. Then I realized that any decision pertaining to not having this baby was wrong but I did not want a child with this man! What in the hell was I going to do? I began to pray, "Lord please do not let me be pregnant!" My heart began racing, my stomach hurt and I became nauseous. The nurse then

Standing on my Healing: From Tainted to Chosen

walks in and closes the door behind her. With excitement in her face and in her tone she says, "It's positive!! You're pregnant!!", and immediately I screamed, "NO!" then broke down and cried. She asked me why I was not happy and I told her, "I will never get away from him now! I do not want to have his baby!" I don't even remember what she said to me next. I just remember being sent to the desk where pregnant women set up appointments, I saw him and got even angrier. The ghetto girl at the reception desk says all loud and out of place, "Girl you pregnant! Congratulations!". I told her to shut up and just schedule my next appointment. She hands me my appointment card as I hear the irritating voice of this man with an accent say, "You pregnant? You pregnant? I'm going to be a father!" I looked at him, rolled my eyes and said, "not for long." As we walked to the car he asked me what I meant and if I was leaving. I told him that I was not having his kid and we fussed about it from City Line Avenue all the way back to the North East. When we got in I heard a message from my mom asking me to give her a call so I get myself together and call her. When she answers and realized that it was me she was all happy and said that the doctor's office called for me and told her that I was pregnant. I was furious!! What nerve do they have telling my personal business? It is confidential! Her entire mood changed as I began to curse, cry and tell her how unhappy I was. The rest of the conversation is a blur but I do remember changing doctors after that.

My life seemed to always be a hot mess. I knew there were people who had it worse than I could even imagine and would especially love to have a baby but this was bad for me. When am I ever going to be happy and enjoy the good life like I always fantasized about? I cannot honestly say I remember everything that occurred from the time I received the positive pregnancy test. All I know is that I was always sick, not just morning sickness but there was

Standing on my Healing: From Tainted to Chosen

more going on inside. Vomiting constantly was an understatement, the diarrhea, shortness of breath, chest pains and weakness plus my stomach was constantly hurting and I cried all the time. It was time for me to go back to the doctors and see what was really going on. I never wanted him going to the doctor with me so I made sure to schedule appointments when he was already at work and let him know when it was too late for him to take off work or better yet, not tell him at all. One day I had an appointment for a full checkup and I was scared out of my mind when they told me that I could be having twins, my baby was really big, or the fibroid tumors were really growing. My options were to have an abortion then remove the tumors, keep the baby and operate later (that is if the baby and I survived); they could not guarantee what would actually happen. I opted for an abortion which they tried to talk me out of but I stood my ground and asked what the cost was. Upon finding out that the procedure fee was almost $400 and I barely had $40 to my name I knew that it was time go into grind mode to get the funds I needed. I did attempt to ask the guy I was with for the money and tell him it was for something else but he said that I was lying. All he would say is that he knew I was going to kill his baby because every woman that he got pregnant got an abortion. WHAT? Are you kidding me? What have I gotten myself into?

I was still attending barber school but it was tough since I had to be there sometimes at 7:30am and I would be so sick during that time. I pressed though especially since he drove me every single day; there was no time away from this man. He would not allow me to do anything that did not involve him taking me there and picking me up. He did not want me out of his sight unless he was at work and I was at school. I was able to catch the bus home after school because he was still at work but that was the only time I had peace from him. One day I really needed my

Standing on my Healing: From Tainted to Chosen

hair done which I normally kept done all the time since I was in barber school and I did hair but the severity of the sickness kept me weak and not able to do it myself. I asked my daughter's godmother to do my hair one day and she said she would braid it for me so that I would not have to do anything to it for a while. I scheduled for her to do it on a Saturday at my mom's house so that I could see my family too which he kept me from. I asked him if he would drop me off to my mom's which was about fifteen minutes away. He said, "No, let's go to Dorney Park". I told him that I thought it was too late in the morning to go and we should go next weekend like 7:00am when it was not so crowded. Now since I had known this man he never cursed at me or raised his voice so what happened next shocked me. He got in my face and said, "B%^$# I'll kill you if you leave! You're not going anywhere!!". I guess I should have been afraid especially since he had guns all over the house like in drawers, under the bed and even under his pillow. Me, afraid? Not cocky Lee! I told him I wish he would even think about it because by the time he grabbed one of those guns I will have already blown his head off! I pushed past him and grabbed the phone to call my mom. While I was doing that he takes the key out of the deadbolt of the front door which meant that I was locked in. I called my mom yelling in the phone for her to come and get me while he is yelling in the background saying that I am not going anywhere.

For over 10 years I had been a witness to domestic violence so there is no way that the cycle will repeat with me! It had to stop somewhere and this day I had determined that it would stop with me. Seeing some of the things I saw as a child helped me to not take death threats lightly. I did not doubt for a moment that he was serious but for some reason I was not afraid. It appeared to be forever before my mother showed up so during my wait I packed me and my daughter's clothes. Even when my mom banged on the door this nut would not let me out! After

Standing on my Healing: From Tainted to Chosen

about five minutes and a few threats from my mom and her boyfriend this guy opens the door just enough to push me out of it, then he threw my things out after me. Needless to say, the next few weeks after I left him he came to my mom's house apologizing, offering me his entire paycheck and a bag of granny smith apples which were my favorite; you would have thought an unemployed homeless pregnant single mom would go for it. Are you kidding me? NEVER! I deserved better and I was just so through with being treating like I was worth nothing. For the next five months, this man stalked me! I am talking calling me and telling me what I wore, who I was with, where I went and even sometimes what I ate. When I left the house, he was there and when I got a job he would come and sit outside, making sure that I saw him when I went in and when I came out. The stalking was serious but I did not know how serious until he told me on two occasions that after I had the baby if I did not get back with him he would take my child from me and no one would ever see me again.

Even with the stalking and the threats I was still not afraid of him but knew I had to protect myself at all times so I began to carry a butterfly knife with me which I could use very well and had no problem using if the situation presented itself. In the beginning of this pregnancy I was very angry and did not want to go through with it but how many know that I had a praying grandmother! My grand mom would call me almost daily to check on me and pray with me about my situation. It was no secret as to what was going on because I told her. I did not know God at that time in my life but I knew God through her. She always knew exactly what to say and when to say it to make me feel comfort and support, even love. I was about six months pregnant and while standing in the kitchen doing dishes I felt my baby move and I began to cry. Now I had felt him move before but this time was different; I felt a mother and child bond that not only made me fall to my knees but caused me to cry out to God for forgiveness for my anger and negative thoughts about being pregnant. That day I fell in love with my child and vowed to protect him and my daughter at all costs from anyone or anything that was trying to hurt them.

Standing on my Healing: From Tainted to Chosen

Reflection 12

Time to Leave Old Things Behind

I eventually saved up enough money to rent a room in North Philadelphia off of Ridge Avenue. I do not remember the name of the street I lived on but I know the house I stayed in was two blocks from the projects. I was afraid of the projects due to the horror stories I heard back in the day so I would never go near them let alone walk past them out of fear. Even though I was only renting a room I was given the biggest room because I had a toddler and one on the way. It was mine and I finally felt safe. The pregnancy was still rough for me as I found later that I had gestational diabetes and needed to go into the hospital for a three-day observation which turned into much longer than that. On my way to the hospital I went into labor on the bus and by the time I got to the hospital and in my room I was definitely in labor; I was a little over 6 months pregnant. I was put on various monitors which confirmed the condition that I was in but I was not ready to have this baby and he certainly was not developed enough to be delivered. I told them to do whatever they could to keep me from having him and to keep us both healthy. They put me on hospital bedrest for two weeks which meant that if I had to go to the bathroom a nurse gave me a urinal, when I needed bathing a nurse had to come bath me. I was not allowed to get out of the bed for anything, it was humiliating and depressing. One day while lying in the bed I realized that I had to give my baby a name in case he decided he did not want to wait any longer. I opened the drawer next to my bed and found a baby name book, when I opened it the first name I saw meant "prince or ruler". There were different spellings and I chose Amir; I did so for the meaning and not the origin as so many people believe and certainly not for religious reasons because I am a Christian. I named my children based off of what I believed they would be:

Charisma

a personal magic of leadership arousing special popular loyalty or a special magnetic charm or appeal.

Amir

Prince or Ruler

Standing on my Healing: From Tainted to Chosen

I was eventually released from the hospital before I had my baby and missed all but one of my prenatal classes. The doctor scheduled me for delivery on March 9, 1993 at 6am since they could not determine exactly when he was coming. The evening before I was scheduled to go in I sat up watching a movie and felt like I was constipated so I kept going to the bathroom trying to go. I was not able to go and my stomach was hurting so bad I decided to go to sleep. Well, I overslept and when my mom woke me it was about 7am so I got ready to go to the hospital. I told her that I had to go to the bathroom and after taking so long she asked me was I alright, I told her my stomach hurt and I needed to move my bowels. She said, "Alicia are you pushing?" I told her I was because I had to go and she said, "NO, you are in labor come on girl!" I got up and we sped to the hospital. When we got there the doctor had everything prepared but I was so afraid and in pain. A nurse came in to give me an epidural and I told her if she tried to stick me with that mess that I would snatch it from her and stick her with it! "Heck no you are not stabbing me in my back as a matter of fact I don't want any drugs at all I will do this naturally!" After fussing and giving them a hard time my doctor came in and talked me into allowing them to put just a little pain reliever in my I.V. which I believe at the time was Demerol because my heart rate and blood pressure was getting too high due to the pain; I just did not want my baby drugged. When it was time to give birth I remember them telling me to give them one more push which is what I did. I was exhausted but when I gave them that last push, my vagina locked around my baby's neck causing him to lose oxygen and he began to turn blue. Without any anesthesia the nurse cut my vagina from front to back and got my son out. OUCH!!!! Yeah I know, it is graphic but hey that is what happened. While they were stitching me I kept telling them I had to go to the bathroom but they insisted it was just pressure I was feeling. I told them it was not pressure but I had to go to the bathroom really bad. They finished the stitches, let me see my son and then helped me to the bathroom. Oh yeah, I had to really go and the pain was beyond words! I would rather have had another baby then go to the bathroom in that moment; I was in there yelling and crying and it hurt so bad but I was relieved when I was finally finished. My beautiful baby boy Amir DeShawn was born Tuesday, March 9, 1993 at 2:11pm weighing 7lbs 5 ½ ounces. I was so happy and he was an angel sent to me from God! After a few days of observation, I was free to go home and I did not have diabetes - baby Diggs and Mom were healthy.

Pregnant women who have never had diabetes before but who have high blood glucose (sugar) levels during pregnancy are said to have gestational diabetes. to According to a 2014 analysis by the Centers for Disease Control and Prevention, the prevalence of gestational diabetes is as high as 9.2%. The placenta supports the baby as it grows. Hormones from the placenta help the baby develop. But these hormones also block the action of the mother's insulin in her body. This problem is called insulin resistance. Insulin resistance makes it hard for the mother's body to use insulin. She may need up to three times as much insulin (American Diabetes Association, 1995-2016; CDC, 2014).

Within days my ex found out that I gave birth to his son so he kept calling my mom's house but I would not talk to him. For over a month I kept getting prank calls from someone telling me they were watching me and even though he did not have my new number at home, I felt certain that it was him or someone he had to call me. One day I was in the park and when I got home I received another prank call telling me what I wore, what I did and how beautiful my children were. That was it. By the time my baby got his first set of shots I knew I had to make a

Standing on my Healing: From Tainted to Chosen

life changing decisions for my children and I. One day he called me while I was at my mom's and asked to see my son but he messed up when he said that if the baby is definitely his and I did not make the decision to be back with him then he would take my baby and no one would see me again. Ok so here we go with this mess again. I told him that he could come by that Saturday morning to see his son at 8:00am but that Friday at 8:00am I was on the road to Virginia. Many would probably say that was wrong to not let him see his kid but I was thinking about the safety of my children and I. You have no idea what you would do unless you are put in that situation and I certainly was not taking any chances of him taking my baby or "making sure no one would see me again" as he put it. At age 22 I left from my home state to live in Waynesboro, Virginia.

According to statistics from John Carroll University, people ages 18-24 experience the highest rate of stalking. One in 6 women and one in 19 men in the United States experience stalking during their lifetime. During a 12month period an estimated 14 in every 1,000 persons age 18 or older wer3e victims of stalking. 66.2% of female victims of stalking were stalked by a current or former intimate partner. 31% percent of women stalked by former intimate partners are sexually assaulted by their stalker. Three in 10 victims reported being injured emotionally or psychologically from being stalked and the average duration of stalking is 1.8 years (JCU, n.d.)

Standing on my Healing: From Tainted to Chosen

Standing on my Healing: From Tainted to Chosen

Reflection 13

Whirlwind

Coming from the fast paced city I did not enjoy Waynesboro one bit. While I did make friends and had some fun, I was totally unhappy but had to make the best of a bad situation even though I got caught up in some things that were not becoming of me. I worked two jobs to take care of my babies and attempted to save money to move as soon as I could. I was determined that I would go back to Philly and try to make a life for my children and I, but where would I go and how would I get back there? Over time, I eventually was back in touch with my daughter's father whom I loved even though the relationship was not healthy. How many know that when you are in bondage to self and other people you go back to familiar people, places and things. I did not have a phone so we were writing letters back and forth. I told him how I felt and he said that I could come back and live with him and his grandmother. I knew deep down that it was not a good idea but I sure did not want to stay where I was. One day while at a convenience store I saw an old couple with a pickup truck. I took a deep breath and got up the nerve to stop them and ask them for a ride to Philadelphia. I told them my story and said I only had $250.00 but I would give them every dime if they would just take me back. To my surprise they agreed! I needed a couple of weeks to get everything prepared so we set up a date for them to come pick me up. I only packed my children's clothes and my clothes, let my friends and mother know I was leaving and back to Philly I went. The couple accepted $200.00 from me and told me to keep $50 for myself. Here I am a 22 year old single mother of two children who left my home town to go to

Standing on my Healing: From Tainted to Chosen

another state running from a stalker just to return to my home state to be in a dead end relationship with my first love; I guess that I had not had enough pain and heartache in my life.

From Philly to Waynesboro Virginia, back to Philly then to Newport News Virginia and Norfolk Virginia all within a two-year span proved to be a life of instability. When I moved to Virginia again I made the decision to take my daughter's father with me not just because he was my first love but mainly because I did not want my daughter to grow up without her father in her life. Plus, I thought if he moved from his environment then he would be a better man and really step up as a father. You cannot change a person regardless to where you take them or what you do but instead they have to want to change for themselves. Well, I was not thinking like that then. I was insecure and had no identity of my own to even be on my own; all I really knew was him. Of course moving to Norfolk and Newport News did not change anything in our relationship. We were still off and on, always argued, and he continued to step out on me with other females. The last time we split up I really thought it would have been for good. I was finally actually happy and gaining some true independence. I worked two jobs to get my own apartment and care for my children, I really felt good about myself.

During my stay in Newport News I became really close friends with this girl I worked with and we seemed to be inseparable. We walked home together from work every day, our children played together, we talked about everything and I spent a lot of time with her and her Husband; they were my family. One day she and I made plans to go clothes shopping when we got off work and I could not wait until the end of the day to hang with my sister girl. After work I rushed home to get showered and dressed for our shopping trip and was so excited. When I got in my phone kept ringing off the wall so I decided to answer it. On the other end was a friend of

Standing on my Healing: From Tainted to Chosen

mine who really never called me like that but they knew this one thing: I was not the type to beat around the bush. When I answered he said, "Alicia, Mardwena died this morning". I was in total shock and knew he was not lying. I hung up the phone and sprinted to her apartment which was about ten minutes from where I lived. Her husband and children were there and very upset along with other family and he told me that she had a brain aneurysm. I knew she complained about having headaches but both her and I thought it was just from lack of rest because we both worked two jobs. I was devastated! I have never been so close to a friend and then lose them so suddenly. That sadness was like none other and I went into a depression which resulted in me losing one of my jobs. During this sad time in my life I was weak and vulnerable only to find myself in the arms of my first love yet again. He always knew what to say to me to win me over; I thought he loved me so much and he was apologetic enough to be better. He held me every night as I cried in his arms and very quickly he stole my heart which obviously he always had.

While he and I were apart, I really did not have any true male prospects except this one handsome and respectful gentleman who was in the military, but he lost his life in an airplane crash. I guess it was meant for me to be with the only one I have known to love since I was fifteen years old. What I thought was a good thing, ended faster than I could blink. Before I knew it he was cheating like he always did, wasting money that should have been for bills and rent. The next thing I knew, we were being evicted yet again. I then made a decision to go into the military because I thought it would help me become a more stable parent so that I could care for my children properly. I contacted my father and asked him to keep my children so that I could enlist; he agreed but asked me to come to North Carolina to see how I would like it. I thought, "THE COUNTRY!?" I told him I was not ready to live a farm life with cows and

Standing on my Healing: From Tainted to Chosen

horses, which in my ignorance I thought was the case. He lived in High Point, N.C. and told me that it was not country but more like suburbs. I was hesitant because I could not even find that city on the map let alone have ever heard of it but I trusted my daddy and needless to say, homeless and depressed. It could not be as bad as the situation I was in at the time so I agreed, on one condition, that my daughter's father could come. (I know, I know…just hush your pie hole.) I did not want him to come because I felt I could not be without him this time but because I did not want my daughter to be without her dad and I honestly felt obligated to take him with us because he had nowhere to go either. Besides, I did take him from his family in Philly and he did not have anyone in Newport News nor was he employed. Yeah, I know, yet another stupid decision.

Reflection 14

A New Chapter in Life

By age twenty-five I finally let my first love go for good after I moved to North Carolina. The thing is, by the time I did that I was emotionally drained and suicidal. In my head; with the extreme depression, low self-esteem, rejection, and not feeling loved or respected I thought my death would be the best thing for everyone; I just could not take anymore. Now you have people who believe in God, some who do not, some who believe in the devil, some who do not and then there are those who believe in them both. I am one who believes in both. In December 1997, I kept hearing a voice tell me to kill myself but the awful thing is I was not afraid. I remember saying that my children would be okay with my dad when I was gone. I had convinced myself that their life would be better and more stable if I removed myself from the equation. Now in killing myself I wanted it to be quick with no suffering. I did not have pills to take so I knew that method was not an option and since I did not like guns I knew that was not going to work either. Then here comes the voice in my head giving me details on how I was going to die. Nothing but the devil!!

During a fight in my house between my dad and my ex, the enemy told me to walk outside to the middle of the street and when I got out there a white car would be speeding up the street which would hit me and I would die instantly. As I walked in the street there was not one car out there but then out of nowhere here came this white car speeding up the street! At that point I knew for sure that I am destined to die so I decide to walk, but my legs would not move! I am literally stuck in the middle of the street on the double yellow lines and I cannot move my body! I thought to myself, "Oh my gosh I am going to die!" Miraculously this speeding white car zips past me running the next two red lights but does not hit me because I was frozen in place. Once the car passes me I was no long stuck but I am in tears so I cross the street, fall to the ground in a fetal position screaming and crying. "I can't even kill myself!" I was crying like I have never cried before and everything else from there is a blur. What I do remember next is hearing a man's voice say, "Baby what's wrong?", but I could not see him through my tears, all I could see were red and blue burry lights from the police who showed up. I tell him, "I just want Jesus to come and take me away! I wanna die!". Next I hear the man say, "Back up man!" The next voice says, "That is my sister man!" I do not remember the rest of the night, it is literally a blur but I do know that was the last time that I saw my baby's dad.

After finally getting out of the 10 year relationship I was in, getting away from suicidal thoughts and escaping severe depression, I finally felt like a normal person. I rededicated my life back to the Lord and could be a productive mother and woman again. I realized in 1998 that my children were not mine but instead they were gifts from God and it was time for me to appreciate what God has allowed me to be, a mother. It took time to get out of the fussing and cussing mode of parenting but I must say, I was happy and beginning to get myself together. So many things had happened overtime that I really kind of forgot much of it.

Reflection 15

Back to Philly, Again

While writing this book I stopped several times and let anywhere from 4 months to almost a year go by without writing. There were several things in my life that triggered my desire to write a book and even though there were many things that I got through, the next few pages were extreme turning points in my life. So much has happened in the next 12 years that sometimes I do not even know where to start. With that being said, I will take it a page at a time.

I started working at APAC (UPS Customer Service) in September 1997, I made pretty good money, had full benefits and met lots of people. Working full time and being a full time mom was not easy, especially without a car but I did not know how to drive. Living in Philly all of my life I was used to walking, catching the bus, or the subway. The bottom line was that I needed a car to have more freedom to do other things and especially so that I could have more time with my children. After walking them to day care at 6am, catching the bus to my shuttle then the shuttle to work for eight to ten hours, then turn around and do the same thing to get home, by the time I did get home there was enough time to get my kids ready for bed just to get up and do it all over again. After doing that for almost two years I knew there was something else that I could be doing with my life to make it better for my children besides going to work and just coming home. So I made a decision to go to college.

Standing on my Healing: From Tainted to Chosen

Making the decision to go to college was very frightening because it had been a very long time since I had finished high school, plus I honestly did not think I was smart enough to even go to college. Even though that low self esteem spirit came up and tried to choke the life out of me, with the encouragement of friends and family I stepped out on faith and took a chance. I was absolutely clueless as to what I wanted to go to school for but after a little researching and thinking about things that I like to do, I chose computer programming. I did not realize it until after I was registered and already taking a few classes that computer repair is actually what I wanted to do. I decided to stay in the field I was in because I already signed up for it and I just may have been pretty good at it, so information systems it is. It turned out to be pretty cool and interesting for the first two years; I received an 'A' in every class each semester except for that dag on math. (I always said math was from the devil and I was going to defeat it! lol) I pressed through all the while encouraging myself that I could get through it. Information systems was a real challenge for me especially when we got to the part of writing code, RPG, COBOL, etc., blah blah blah. I got through some of the code writing with no problem but as I advanced it got so hard. I love learning new things and I do not even mind challenges but this right here was way over my head.

I started school in 2000 and in 2001 my family was planning a family reunion: Diggs, Johnson, Robinson Family Reunion 2001. This was my dad's side of the family whom I did not know that well, since I was not raised with him, so I was a little excited and looking forward to meeting people who were a part of me. At first I did not want to go but my dad's wife kindly talked me in to it, even mentioning that I may even find my husband in Philly.

Standing on my Healing: From Tainted to Chosen

Proverbs 18:22

He who finds a wife finds and good thing and obtains favor from the Lord.

That was really a joke to me at the time because I really was not interested in having a relationship with anyone. I had those feelings even though I had been purposely practicing abstinence because I was waiting to be found by that special someone who would be proud to call me his wife. You see, after being in unsuccessful relationships and having flings that made no sense I felt that it was best to just wait so that it was right the next (and final) time. I really wanted to be the woman of God that I was created to be, or at least who I thought I was created to be. Anyway, going to this reunion would give me the opportunity to visit Philly again and to meet family.

Standing on my Healing: From Tainted to Chosen

Standing on my Healing: From Tainted to Chosen

Reflection 16

My High School Sweetie

It was actually a great idea since I had a new car by 2001 after I totaled my first car in a tire blow out about a year before. I was not badly hurt but I thank God that my children were not with me because my son would not have survived since he sat on the rear passenger side which was absolutely destroyed from me hitting a utility pole. Anyway, since I had my new car I would be taking the eight hour drive for the first time alone. My children and I made it safely after twelve hours. My dad wanted me to stop and rest every two hours plus call since it was my first long distance drive alone. We got there on June 31 and stayed until July 5 since the reunion was scheduled for July 4. It was so great seeing family I did know and meeting family I did not know. I even took my children to every neighborhood I lived in, every school I attended and all of my main hangouts. In my early teens I lived in Germantown on Locust Ave. and my late teens on Church Lane. My old high school sweetheart lived on Church Lane at one point so I decided to go there and say hello. He was not there but I left my name and number with his dad who could care less that I was there, but he did relay the message to him and his sister whom I was very close to. I was really surprised to get their call so when I did I drove from South Philly to Olney to see them. We were all happy to see each other and meet each other's children. I talked with my home girl for a while and then chilled with my ex for the rest of the time I was there.

Standing on my Healing: From Tainted to Chosen

When we were teens we would sit up for hours and talk about any and everything. We did that same thing on July 2, 2001. We reminisced, laughed and held each other outside on the steps as we did years ago until the sun came up. By 6 a.m. I needed to get back to my aunt's house to shower and change to meet the family for our day at the Philadelphia Zoo by 8 a.m.! I think I made it to the zoo and 8:30 a.m. which was when everyone else showed up and I was more than exhausted! Every time we stopped for the kids to look at something I sat down somewhere to close my eyes; I was so miserably sleepy and at the time losing so much sleep was so worth it.

July 4, 2001 was the cookout and reunion in the park and it was so great! In the beginning I did not want to go to Philly because I did not know my dad's side. I was worried about feeling left out and different from everyone else but instead everything turned out so totally different than I thought it would. I had a feeling of wholeness when I was with some of the family I already knew and when I met the others. Being around family I looked like, sounded like, and acted like was more than I could have ever asked for. We all exchanged numbers and stayed in touch as much as our different lives allowed us to.

Once my children and I returned back to our lives in North Carolina, my ex and I talked on the phone constantly and wrote letters to each other almost every week! (Yes we wrote letters- not texting and even though I had an email address and a computer, he did not, so writing and talking on the phone for hours was the thing to do.) I remember him writing a letter to me saying how much he loved me and wanted to spend the rest of his life with me. I really felt like

Standing on my Healing: From Tainted to Chosen

he was the one not just because we had known each other since I was fourteen but also since I prayed and told God that I believed I would be married by the time I turned thirty and I was twenty-nine! Now I will keep it real, I *felt* like he was the 'one' but I was not sure. See, during that time I was visiting him in July while in Philly, I literally heard the voice of God tell me that it was time to go. I just kept saying 'okay I am about to', but inside I was having so much fun. I continued to talk instead of leaving. A while later I heard again, "Alicia it is time to leave"; I ignored the voice. The third time I heard the voice of God tell me it was time to go, me thinking I knew everything and responding in the flesh, I silently said, "But God the kids fell asleep, I do not want to wake them and it is not respectful for me to come in to my aunt's house late to wake her just to let us in.". After that I did not hear anything else.

After my ex told me he wanted to spend the rest of his life with me I wrote him to explain how my life revolved around church and pleasing God. I told him I was a Christian and was not the same person I was years ago. I asked him if he believed in God because I accepted Jesus Christ as my Lord and Savior and I want to be with a man who loves God. He agreed that he "believed in God and loved God". Notice I just asked him if he believed in and loved God, I never confirmed if he accepted Christ as Lord and Savior which is a part of my spiritual belief and lifestyle. Going by my flesh and emotions I became excited! He and I spoke on the phone about a future together, he said he would quit his job and move to North Carolina with my children and I to start over. I was so overjoyed and just knew I was making the right decision though a little hesitant about 'shacking up" but we are going to get married quickly so it would not be too bad; right?

Standing on my Healing: From Tainted to Chosen

See, as I stated before, I just ran into him again on July 2, 2001 after not seeing him since 1992 and here it was approximately the middle of July and we were discussing him dropping his life in Philly and moving to North Carolina; looking back on it now that seemed like it was a little too soon. Did we know each other well enough to do this? Were we both ready? How would my children feel about this drastic change? It has always been the three of us since 1997! Well, I sat my children down and spoke to them about the huge decision I was about to make. Their response at the time was that they liked him and it was ok with them that we get together as long as I was happy. It was settled. He and I made plans for him to move to North Carolina with us and start our new life.

Reflection 17

Listen to 'The' Voice

It was important for me to talk with my children about this decision because it would be affecting them too. Many times as parents we do not talk with our children and ask them how they feel about certain things that pertain to their lives and we do not listen to them when it comes to certain things. Yes, it is our job to make decisions for them until they are old enough to make them for themselves but it is still important to ask how they feel sometimes especially when huge life altering decisions are made. Now, would I have made the decision to be with this man if they had said they did not like him; unfortunately I probably would have. My daughter was eleven years old and my son was eight years old during this time, I simply wanted to make sure they were happy but I wanted to be happy also. I wanted to provide a stable home for them that had loving parents; I wanted them to feel loved and protected. Little did I know I was actually giving them the opposite but did not know it because I was so blind.

I heard a voice say," Do not allow him to move in". I felt like the voice was not God and it had to be the enemy not wanting me to be happy. I was confused and scared. I had been waiting almost two years for my husband (as if that was a long time) and believed God that I would be married by age thirty and I was twenty-nine so it had to be right. My children seemed to be alright with it and my 'flesh' said it was right. I told my dad and his wife; they were not that thrilled but said that they would support my decisions and love me just the same. One day

Standing on my Healing: From Tainted to Chosen

while riding home from work with a minister friend that I was very close with, I shared my recent decisions with her. She got upset with me and said, "NO ALICIA! This does not feel right!" I told her that it was right and I loved him. She then stated, "This is not right, what if he is sick?!". I raised my voice and said, "Then I will take care of him! Why can't you be happy for me?" See, she had never ever raised her voice before or been angry around me so I was shocked by her response and mood change, yet still blind and unable to read between the lines. I told her that it was too late because he had already moved in and we were getting married. I asked her to attend the wedding but she refused. I got out of her car and attempted to say something to her but she sped off before I could even close the door. I was crushed, angry, confused and even afraid because I trusted her wisdom. Why would she say he could be sick and why was she wishing bad on him?

Once I got in the door I did not mention the conversation I had just had with my friend. When I got in the dinner was done, the children's homework was complete, they were eating and the house was clean. To me, he was my knight in shining armor; I never ever thought that I would have a love like that! While eating dinner he asked me if he and I were getting married on his birthday, which was in March, or my birthday, which was in February, so I said mine and he suggested February 14. I told him I did not think anyone would come because it was Valentine's Day and my birthday was on a weekday, so we chose Saturday, February 23, 2002 which was five days after my birthday. I was so stoked and knew that I was in love!!

Standing on my Healing: From Tainted to Chosen

My friend called me later that evening to plead with me not to go through with what I was planning. I told her about the date and she sighed then told me that she would keep the kids and I in her prayers, she loved me and she hung up. My heart sunk. I told my fiancé about everything we discussed and he said to forget her – that she is jealous and probably wanted me for herself. I got upset and told him that she was not like that, she loves me and the children and she was just concerned. I explained that she had always been there for us and did not want to see us hurt but he insisted that she just did not know him. That night I did not sleep well; I could only think about my friend being upset and I heard a voice tell me not to marry this man.

There are many time that we have clues to make decisions in our life or not make decisions and it is up to us to really analyze what is good for our future but most importantly we have to recognize the difference between the voice of God, the enemy and our selves.

John 10:27 (NKJV)

My sheep hear My voice, and I know them, and they follow Me.

Standing on my Healing: From Tainted to Chosen

Reflection 18

Don't Marry This Man!

The wedding plans were being made and I was so excited. My ring was beautiful and the new relationship we were both starting seemed to be going great. Before my fiancé came into my life I was active in the church I was attending at the time, I was on the choir, the praise team, the tape ministry and the radio ministry. Since I was 'shacking up' I made an appointment to speak with the Pastor and I told him I wanted to be relieved of my ministerial duties since I knew what I was doing was not in line with how things were done there. I would not be allowed to serve on a ministry because I was living out of wedlock. I later asked my pastor for pre-marital counseling which was protocol before marriage takes place. We all arranged to meet at his home and during the meeting it was suggested that my fiancé and I live in different households until we got married. We would have been willing to do that if he had his own place, as a matter of fact we would have done that first but financially that was not an option for us. Since we were unable to make that happen, the pastor refused to marry us. He and his wife told my fiancé that I was a very beautiful, smart and loving woman and to take good care of me and not hurt me, then we left.

So here we go, yet another disappointment so far especially since I really desired a wedding in a church. My fiancé said that we should just go to the justice of the peace but I insisted that I wanted an actual wedding. I wanted the dress, the ceremony, the reception - it was a dream for me and I still did not see the signs that were right in front of my face. I spoke with my dad and his wife about it and even though they too had mixed feelings about this union, they supported me and agreed to help. They found a recreation center that was spacious enough for us to have a ceremony there. My fiancé and I went downtown to the justice of peace to register and asked the magistrate if she could do the ceremony outside of the courthouse. She agreed. I was getting happy all over again and things were starting to look up. Now to find a dress!

My fiancé moved in with my children and I at the end of July 2001 (yes it was just weeks after we met up again after not seeing one another for 9 years.) Oh how we want everything to be at microwave speed and then wonder why later things just did not go the way we planned them.

One day in August 2001, I was in class working a program on the computer and it was freezing especially since I was sitting right under a vent. Before the class was over I was shivering, coughing, and sneezing. By the time I got home I checked my temperature and I had a fever. After a few days went by my throat was hurting badly and I just could not kick the fever that I had so I decided to go to the doctor's office. They determined that I had strep and a cold so I was given a prescription and was sent home. A week goes by and I was vomiting, had diarrhea really bad and felt weak with body aches and pains. I went back to the doctors after vomiting up blood. I was given more pills to control the vomiting since my esophagus was getting damaged from the vomiting; I felt miserable and was losing so much weight. I stayed away from my children so that I would not make them sick. Needless to say, my family was very concerned and so was I.

About another week or so later I begin to feel well enough to eat and go back to school and work. Even though I was not vomiting and longer or running to the bathroom, the fever was gone and my throat no longer hurt. I did notice that my lymph nodes in my neck were swollen and my neck hurt when I turned my head. What the heck is the matter with me now? Being the researcher that I am I started to look up the symptoms that I had. After a few hours of searching I found lymphoma cancer on the website of cancer.org and it explained that Lymphoma is a cancer that starts in the cells that are part of the body's immune system. I had all of the symptoms but I wanted to be sure so I schedule another appointment. My doctor told me that I should not worry because it was probably nothing but I knew it was something because I knew my body. I had annual exams without missing any of them, got tested for HIV and other STDs every three to six months with negative test results and my tubes were tied so I knew I was not pregnant. Before my fiancé came into my life I had been practicing abstinence for almost two years, I had been tested for HIV and other STDs and again in the beginning of August 2001 I was tested.

Anyway, it was mid-September and I could not get an appointment until December. That was a long time to wait for an appointment for a biopsy but there was not much I could do but wait. My appointment was scheduled for December 13, 2001 at 10am and I figured since they were booked up they would possibly have to refer me to a specialist. I was concerned with my health but I was also worried about getting a dress for my wedding. I wanted it to be unique yet inexpensive; it needed to be white for purity with purple for royalty plus purple is my favorite color. My dad's wife was with me all the time while searching for this dress and it sure was frustrating not being able to find one that worked for me. I was nervous, frustrated and afraid all at the same time.

Am I truly supposed to be marrying this man? If not, how will me and my children's life be with him? How will my family feel? And what the hell is wrong with my neck and this swelling? What if I have cancer? There was so much on mind I could not even think straight; I felt like I was losing myself. The relationship I had with my church family was not the same and I was beginning to feel like an outcast all because I moved in with him first before marriage? Ok, well my children love me and my family has my back.

Standing on my Healing: From Tainted to Chosen

Reflection 19

The Shock of my Life

October and November of 2001 are a total blur for me but the next months following are as clear as the sky is on a nice warm sunny summer's day. December 12, 2001 arrived and I asked my fiancé if he wanted to go with me to the doctors the next day but he says no he would rather stay at the house. Thursday December 13, 2001 was here and I asked him again if he wanted to go, I really wanted him there for support, yet he still insisted on staying home. I left and made it to my appointment before 10am; I spoke to the receptionist and nurses since they were familiar with me. I waited in the waiting room for a much longer time than usual, people were coming after me and being seen yet I was still there. I could see the nurses staring at me but not calling my name so I asked them what the holdup was and they reassured me that someone would be right with me. As I walked back to the waiting room I could vaguely hear side conversation from one of the nurses saying, "I do not want to tell her." Then the other responded," But it's your job you have to tell her." I did not know who they were whispering about but I went and sat down anyway.

Minutes later I hear them calling my beautiful name - "Alicia". I got up mumbling under my breath, "finally". I was taken to a small room which was not where I would normally go but I sat down not questioning the location. The nurse who I knew from past visits did not say anything to me but she had a strange look on her face; a concerned non-communicative look and treated me as if I was not even in the room. The nurse pushed a yellow folder to me that had my name on it. At first I had no idea what I was looking for but then I saw in bold red capital letters: HIV POSITIVE. I began to scream, "NO, NO ,NO!!". I pushed the folder away and got up to leave but she was already at the door holding my purse. I screamed and cried and she just held me allowing me to slump on the floor while screaming uncontrollably and crying. This was the worse day of my life!

What do you do after getting devastating and debilitating news like that? Most Christians and those who believe in healing and miracles would say speak healing, believe you are healed, give it to God, etc. Well, in 2001 I did not know how to speak life, think positive, or believe God for healing. I knew a positive diagnosis was not a death sentence but what I did not know was what my fiancé would say or do, what my family would say or how my babies would feel.

MY BABIES! Who would take care of them if I get sick? Will I live long enough to see them grow up? Will I live to be a grandmother? Oh my gosh I cannot marry this man! What if I passed the virus on to him? How long did I have HIV? Who did I pass the virus to? What am I going to do now?

All of these questions ran through my head while screaming and crying in that little room. I asked the nurse to call my fiancé which she did for about thirty minutes or so, but there was no answer. I was so distraught and there are so many things in my head!

Standing on my Healing: From Tainted to Chosen

Where was he? He smoked cigarettes so he could have been outside, but for that long? The nurse left messages every time she called! He did not know anyone and he was not at work- where in the world was he! I cannot do this alone I just cannot; it is too much!

My heart felt like it was coming out of my chest. I told them to call my step mom; she was the only one I knew who was at home and could support me. About an hour or more passed and my fiancé showed up and I was still crying extremely hard. He held me and with concern asked me what was wrong. Through tears I told him that my test came back positive. In a concerned and empathetic voice he says, "No baby! I am so sorry! We will get through this together!" I then scream, " Not Cancer I have HIV! I have HIV!".

His attitude changed which I did not pay much attention to until after the fact. He responded with a monotone, "oh". I cried more and more and told him that I could not marry him and the wedding was off. His response was that he still wanted us to get married and it will be alright. I told him that I probably infected him and I that I could not bring myself to do this. At that moment a doctor comes in and tries to talk to me but I am still crying uncontrollably. My fiancé then says a in a stern voice, "Be quiet and listen to what the doctor is saying!". What the &^%$ do you mean be quiet!? (That is what I said in to myself as I cut my eye at him while still crying.) Then the doctor proceeds to tell me a few of my steps. The doctor had my fiancé leave while we talked more. The conversation was like listening to Charlie Brown's teacher...womp womp womp womp. I am not sure how far we were into the conversation but eventually my step mom came in. Her face had fear all on it and the doctor left her and I alone. I told her the test

Standing on my Healing: From Tainted to Chosen

results and she begins to cry and hold me. She said, " I asked him what was wrong when I saw him in the waiting room and he said he did not know! I have been out there with him for at least ten to fifteen minutes!" I just cried; I felt so empty and dirty, but more so helpless.

Once she went back to the waiting room I was escorted to another room. I did not want to go in the hall because I knew people could hear me screaming and some were staring at me; the nurses even had sad faces, I was feeling as if my heart and soul was sucked from me. Once I was in the room with I guess a doctor, (she could have been a bridge counselor but I do not remember) she told me she had a few questions to ask me and some information to give me. I remember being asked to list all of the guys I had been intimate with for the past few years. Of the guys I had unprotected sex with in the past few years, there were three: my daughter's father, a fling from three years ago and my fiancé. I gave all the information I had on them and was told that my fiancé would have to be tested. All I could think about was, "who did I infect?".

It is amazing as you write down traumatic situations in your life how many details you begin to remember. The doctor/counselor reassured me that this diagnosis was not a death sentence. Through tears I told her I knew that but how long would I live? She explained how so many were living long and healthy lives and I could do the same. I told her that I think it came from my daughter's father because I was with him on and off for 10 years, he was doing drugs and was promiscuous. I explained to her that I had not been intimate with him since 1997 and I had been practicing abstinence while I wait for marriage. I cried even harder telling her how I will never be able to marry now. "WHO WILL WANT TO BE WITH THE HIV GIRL?" I cried some more and she explained that many couples have succeeded with one being positive and one being negative (serodiscordant). What shocked me were her next statements. "Ms Diggs we cannot tell you the exact day of contraction but what we do know is that you have contracted HIV within the last six months but you are very healthy. You have an extremely low viral load and your CD4 or T-helper count is 740." I still did not feel any better after hearing that.

Wait, the last 6 months?? I have not been with anyone but my fiancé in almost two years! No! There is no way he knew and did not tell me!!

Standing on my Healing: From Tainted to Chosen

Standing on my Healing: From Tainted to Chosen

Reflection 20

HIV 101

What is HIV?

Human Immunodeficiency Virus, which is the virus that causes AIDS, Acquired Immunodeficiency Syndrome. According to aids.gov here is the breakdown:

Human- this particular virus can only inflict human beings.

Immunodeficiency- HIV weakens your immune system by destroying important cells that fight disease and infection. A "deficient" immune system cannot protect you.

Virus- a virus can only reproduce itself by taking over a cell in the body of its host.

Your immune system can clear most viruses out of the body but not when it comes to HIV. Once you have HIV you have it for life. Your immune system has T-cells or CD4 cells that the virus attacks to destroy them and make copies of itself to destroy your immune system. I like to call T-cells or CD4 cells your soldiers that fight off infections or the enemy. If your soldiers/CD4 are defeated overtime the virus/enemy causes your immune system to break down making it difficult to fight off infections and diseases. Once that occurs this can lead to AIDS which is the final stage of HIV infection.

What is AIDS?

Acquired- AIDS is not inherited from your parents. You acquire AIDS after birth.

Immuno- Your body's immune system includes all organs and cells that work to fight off infection or disease.

Standing on my Healing: From Tainted to Chosen

Deficiency- You are AIDS defined when your immune system is "deficient" or isn't working the way it should to fight off disease and infection.

Syndrome- A syndrome is a collection of symptoms and signs of disease. AIDS is a syndrome rather than a single disease because it is a complex illness with a wide range of complications and symptoms.

According to the Center for Disease Control and Prevention , HIV is spread through blood, semen (cum), pre-seminal fluid (precum), rectal fluids, vaginal fluids, and breast milk from an HIV infected person. These fluids must come in contact with a mucous membrane, damaged tissue, or be directly injected into the blood stream from a needle or syringe for transmission to possibly occur. HIV does not survive long outside the human body (such as on surfaces) and it cannot reproduce. It is not spread by air or water, insects including mosquitoes or ticks, saliva, tears or sweat. There is no documented case of HIV being transmitted through spitting, casual contact like shaking hands or sharing dishes, toilet seats, closed mouth kissing or social kissing. . You can find other information on the following sites:

www.cdc.gov

www.aids.gov

www.avert.org

www.mayoclinic.org

www.niaid.nih.gov

You can also ask your physician or also contact your local STD testing site. Testing is confidential and beneficial. KNOW YOUR STATUS AND PROTECT YOURSELF!

Reflection 21

More Devastation

He loves me, maybe he just did not know. Well, he got tested while I got resources and set up with a counselor. Before my step mom left the doctor's office she told me that I would have to tell my dad because she could not. She told me that they would be at my house when he got off of work. I did not want her to call him while he was working because I did not want him to worry or be upset while at work. She hugged me, said she loved me and that she would be in my corner, then she left. Shortly after, my fiancé and I left the office. I do not remember all of the details from the doctor's office to the house but I do remember the complete silence shared between my fiancé' and I. December 13, 2001 was a miserable day for me and I still had to tell my dad that I had HIV; man that was so hard. My children were not around, they were at my dad's house so they did not know yet. My dad had tears in his eyes and an extremely angry look on his face as I told him about my diagnosis and explained what HIV was. It is really hard to remember that evening after I told my father, but I do remember him hugging me tight and saying that he loved me before he walked out of the door. My father and his wife were so very angry but they still gave me as much support as they could. They both felt like my fiancé gave me HIV on purpose and that he knew he was infected and did not tell me, but I loved him so much and felt that he loved me enough that he would not do something like that to me unknowingly.

Standing on my Healing: From Tainted to Chosen

I was so depressed and had even stopped going to church especially because during the time I was sick; only two people from the church called to check up on me. My church at that time was a real family to me before I got involved with my fiancé and I felt that I lost them when he and I got together. Initially I did not feel that I was going to die and my life was over but I was more afraid of going through life living with HIV. I was afraid that I was not going to be around to take care of my children or either someone was going to have to take care of me until I died. He had to wait two weeks for his results which would come back during the Christmas holiday therefore he did not get his test results until after the new year in 2002. During the wait I researched, cried, sunk into depression and asked him questions. I wanted to know if he was shooting up drugs, prostituting at one time, highly promiscuous or not using protection and even if he had unprotected sex with men. The more questions I asked the more tense the situation got. I did not want my children to know so whenever he would raise his voice or my questioning turned into the beginning of an argument I would just shut down. I am sure many people feel like they would react different by fighting him, cussing him out etc., but I tell you this, you never know how you will react to a situation until you are actually in it. I wanted to protect my children, I was afraid, I was angry, I felt dirty, tainted, disgusting like HIV was written all over my face and everyone could see it. There were times that I would scrub my body so hard while bathing wishing that I could wash "it" off of me but "it" was in my body and in my blood. I cried so much at night that when I woke up my eyes would be puffy and red. " I can do this, I will be ok." That is what I kept telling myself hoping that sooner or later I would believe it.

Since my fiancé still wanted to get married and I had already sent out the wedding invitations I had to focus as well as keep my mind occupied, so I continued to plan the wedding.

Standing on my Healing: From Tainted to Chosen

You may ask, "Are you really going to marry him and continue on with this wedding?". Sure, why not? Nobody is going to want me anyway. Who would dare want to be with the HIV girl? I am tainted. I am dirty. I am scarred and worthless. I may as well stay with him since he wants me. I will just take care of him and he will take care of me if we get sick. Many say what they would have done in my situation but no, you have no earthly idea what you would actually do when faced with devastating news like this. I had two small children so I had to press on the best way that I knew how.

The time came for him to get his test results so we both went together to the health department. He got his test results and when I asked him what they were he says to me with an attitude, "They are positive, what did you think?". Inside I am falling apart and ready to pass out but I take a deep breath and tell him that it is important for him to keep record of his labs which contain his viral load and cd4. He then goes into a room to talk to a counselor and go through the same steps that I did. When he was finished we left and I asked him what his CD4 and viral load was, he told me that he was not sure about the viral load but that his CD4 was a little over five hundred. I had to go across the street to another business so we walked over there. As we walked quietly my gut said, " Alicia he is lying! Girl you better get that paper work!". I told him that I would hold his envelop in my purse so he did not have to carry it. He said alright and handed me the envelope which I then put in my purse. As we got to the building I told him that I had to go to the bathroom and I would be right back. I went into the ladies room and sat in a stall. I slowly opened the envelope and read from the top of the page until I got to the part that read his viral load and CD4. My heart came out of my chest as I read. His CD4 read 150 which is an AIDS diagnosis and his viral load was over 185,000 copies! I sat there for a moment in shock and

Standing on my Healing: From Tainted to Chosen

motionless. I said to myself that there was no way he knew and still asked to marry me; he loves me, he would not do that to me, I had known him since I was fourteen years old!

Realizing that I had been in the bathroom for a while I got up and left. He asked me what was taking me so long and I told him I had to clean my colon (the number 2). I knew what determined an AIDS diagnosis but I was totally in denial about what I saw thinking maybe the 150 is actually a 750. There was no conversation for the rest of the journey back to the house. When I got in I immediately got on the computer to do more research and I even emailed doctors asking the definition of an AIDS diagnosis and cd4 levels as if I did not know; I sat in front of the computer for hours! While in the middle of researching my children came home so I turned off the computer monitor but not the computer. Once I got them prepared to eat dinner I went back to researching but while I was doing that he came up behind me crying. I shut off the computer monitor and took him in the bedroom so my children would not hear him. He sat on the bed and I held him as he cried. I then asked, " Do you know where you contracted the virus from? Were you having lots of unprotected sex? Doing drugs?". He got very angry and said, "How do you know I didn't get it from you?" I replied, " Those numbers on your paper tell that and I was told that I contracted HIV within the last six months and I was only with you!". He gets louder and says, " That doesn't mean SHIT!". I said, "Man be quiet before my kids hear you! It means a lot when your CD4 is 150 which equates to AIDS!" He just cried more and would not say anything else to me. Maybe he did not know he had HIV after all or did he?

Standing on my Healing: From Tainted to Chosen

Reflection 22

Wedding Bliss

Everything leading up to my wedding day is honestly a blur. I remember getting frustrated and angry while searching for a wedding dress that fit my personality.

What was my personality? I do not want to do this; I am so ugly and disgusting!

My step mom was a great help in finding a dress that I liked at David's Bridal. I really looked fabulous in it! It was white with the perfect size train on it and it made me feel like a queen even though I really felt worthless and dirty. Her cousin made the vail and flowers which were all so pretty. It felt good to have the love and support that I had from my family even though they were hurting and angry about the entire ordeal. My step mother and my father did not want me to marry him and they were the only ones in my family that knew about our diagnosis but they still supported my decision. I tried to pray and kept hearing God tell me not to marry him but I made the decision to do it anyway because I did not want to be alone. The 'busy-ness' from planning the wedding kept my mind off of it but there were still nights that I would wake up crying because of the thought of living with this virus. I would think about how I was always so careful to use condoms or to say no in past relationships but when I got with the man I knew I was going to marry I did not use condoms; I just did not THINK that I had to. I even

Standing on my Healing: From Tainted to Chosen

asked him if he had any sexually transmitted diseases (STDs) and if he had been tested for HIV. He said yes he was tested and did not have anything and I told him I was too and every time I got tested my tests were negative. He agreed his were the same and I believed him. It is so sad that I knew this was not the right thing to do but I felt like it was the only thing to do. Gosh I was so helpless and empty.

The day of my wedding finally came - February 23, 2002 and I was preparing to get married to my high school sweetie who I contracted HIV from - now this is the life (sigh). I kept hearing this voice say, "Do not marry him." What in the world! Is that God? Is it me? No, it has to be the devil! "I will take care of you and you will be okay. Do not marry him." But who is going to want me? I cannot do this alone! I had so many emotions going on that I could not even think straight. I knew in my heart this was not the right thing to do. While I was in the bathroom getting ready I was talking with the ladies and telling them that almost every time a woman gets married she cries and I refuse to cry. All of sudden I burst into tears! I was so scared and drained! I got it together and took a deep breath. As I walked nervously down the aisle with my dad I asked him to hold me tight because I felt like I was going to pass out. I saw friends and family smiling as I walked down and all I can imagine is them saying, "why is she marrying this man? Wow they have HIV!" then I hear the voice, "Do not marry this man!". I was nervous, I was happy I think. I was scared, depressed and confused. I did not know how I felt but what I did know was that I was HIV positive!

Standing on my Healing: From Tainted to Chosen

We said our wedding vows in front of the magistrate with friends and family smiling while looking on. All I could hear was, "Do not marry him!". I was shaking so much you could see my bouquet shaking. We said our 'I dos" and the lights got dim. No one noticed it but me, I looked around at the ceiling as the lights dimmed and realized that I disobeyed the voice of God and just made a huge mistake. God turned His back on me for going forth with a union that was not blessed and was going to destroy my life even more. Yes, I know that God will never leave me nor forsake me (Deut. 31:8 NKJV), but on February 23, 2002 that is what I felt. After the claps and cheers the best part of my wedding occurred. My Broheim, my ace, my pea in a pod, big bro T walked up and began to sing. He did his own version of Lionel Richie's "Truly." I stood there and cried my eyes out smiling as he sang the mess out of that song to me, his sister, with no music just acapela. It was perfect - my big bro made everything okay that day.

Less than a month into the marriage the arguments escalated. I had so many questions that were not answered and I deserved and needed answers. Things got really bad for my children and I when I got married. My husband was verbally, emotionally and mentally abusive and was always angry, drinking and getting high. When I was at work he continued to speak nasty to my children but when I came home he would either leave out of the house or go to sleep. I slipped deeper into depression and even my children started to get depressed and were very unhappy. I hated myself for even allowing my family to suffer because of a man. I hated who I was because I was "infected and dirty." I tried to do things to keep my mind off of the fact that I had this virus in my body but it never helped. I was trying to scrub HIV away while washing, I could not sleep or think straight; I cried a lot and depression was really starting to take more control of me than I wanted it to. I still functioned in school and work while I covered up the

Standing on my Healing: From Tainted to Chosen

things I was going through in my personal life. I lost contact with God and could not talk to Him like I used to even though I never blamed God or asked why me. My dad would tear up every time he saw me which of course made me very uncomfortable. I always felt like someone was looking at me and knew that I was 'tainted'; man it was so dag on hard to deal with.

There were nights that I would jump up out of my sleep because I heard crying which I thought was my children but once I opened my eyes I realized that it was me! Constantly crying in my sleep was getting very old, then I would hear a voice almost every night telling me to kill him. At first I thought that I was tripping, then I realized that it was the enemy whispering those thoughts in my spirit. Even to the point of me hearing the voice as clear as I heard my own self speak. The voice began to get so loud and aggravating to the point that there were times when he was asleep that I wanted to take action on those words. Then, in the midst of all the turmoil I started to hear another voice say to me, "Don't worry I've got your back. I will take care of you." It was so frustrating hearing all of these voices in my head. I just wanted it all to stop. I had to hold on to that positive voice and the safety of my children first.

There were days that my husband and I treated each other as if nothing ever happened. We laughed, we went out, watched movies, and we talked about everything except this HIV diagnosis. One day I came in from work late I was exhausted and I had homework to complete. Well, when I walked in he had an attitude and had been drinking. I think I fed my kids, did all of my motherly duties, they went to bed and then the drama started. I vaguely remember how the argument started and then escalated but we went outside so that we would not wake my kids up.

Standing on my Healing: From Tainted to Chosen

He started accusing me of messing around on him since I was coming home later than usual some nights. I said to him, "I am your wife and I would not cheat plus I have this virus which I got from you and I would never infect anyone like you did to me!". What he said next hit me like a boulder fell on top of me. "Yeah I did it so what!" "Hold up! You said that like you knew you were infected and purposely did this to me!" "Yeah, I knew and I do not care, so what you going to do about it!!" I told him to get out and then I ran in the house and locked the back door but he kicked it in and said he was not going anywhere. I really wanted to kill him right then and there but my babies were in the bedroom asleep and if I took action the way that my flesh wanted me to then I would either go to prison and lose my kids or die trying to take him out and then my kids would be without a mother.

I really do not remember all of the details from that night to the final fight but I do remember the anger building deep in my bones to the point of driving me in sane. I knew that I was going to kill him the first chance that I got I just did not know how and when. I would wake up in the middle of the night ready to do it then I would hear those voices. "Kill him, kill him now while he is sleep", and later, "Wait I got your back!". When I heard the voice, which I knew was God telling me to wait I would say, "What do you mean wait! I cannot wait for you! I have got to kill him!" God would not let me; He had another plan for my life and jail or death was not it. I just did not know how much more of this I could take. This was so much worse than anything I have ever been through in my life. I just did not think that I would survive it.

Standing on my Healing: From Tainted to Chosen

Lee and Uncle Leroy (R.I.P.)

Reflection 23

The Cycle Repeats

I contacted a lawyer and found that I could not just put him out of my house and as far as a divorce, the state of North Carolina says that you have to be legally separated before you can even file for divorce. This is worse than I needed it to be; I just wanted him out of my life. I started to pray to God for a means to get this man completely out of my life without any harm to me or my children or it resulting in my death or jail time; prayer I tell you it really works. God comes right on time and though the results and timing may not be what or how you expect them to be, but God is always on time. It was a nice Saturday morning and for the past week I had been feeling an unusual peace and was extremely nice. I just could not understand the worry I felt but I still kept a positive attitude. The way I felt was so out of the ordinary in spite of the circumstances and it was a little scary for me. Instead of questioning it I just went with it. I got up early on a Saturday morning and made a big breakfast for everyone with so much joy in my heart not even realizing how the day would end. I was even laughing and joking with the man I wanted so much to kill and put out of my house. What in God's name is going on!?

While eating breakfast I decided to sit at the computer, then out of the blue he said to me in a stern voice, "Get up we need to talk!". I said to myself "what in the world just happened?" We all had great breakfast and was just laughing and joking. My youngest sister who was staying with me at the time said, " Oh boy", then her and my daughter went outside on the porch.

Standing on my Healing: From Tainted to Chosen

See, we were all used to his Jekyll and Hyde personality; one moment he would be perfectly fine then the next he would be angry and spazzing out with no explanation! I got up and stepped into the bedroom to see what his issue was. When I walked in he told me I was showing off in front of my sister then he started calling me bad names; I told him that I was going to walk away because I did not have to listen to his bashing. He told me that I better not walk away from him so I reminded him that he was not my father and I was going to do what I wanted. As I started to walk out of the room while holding my plate of food and my orange juice, he closed the door hard which hit me in my back before I was even out of the room! My food and juice flew out of my hand and the fight began!

We were in that bedroom rumbling like two boxers in a ring! I then slipped on the food and hit the floor. While I was down he grabs my hair in his hands and begin to knee me in my head repeatedly. I could hear my daughter screaming and my sister yelling for him to get off of me. It started to get dark as he planted his knee with such force into my head. I launched towards him and tried to get up to no avail. He was seriously trying to hurt me! How could someone say they love you and want to marry you but knowingly infect you with HIV, admit it and then try to bash your head in? This is not the kind of love that I was taught, but it was what I saw the majority of my childhood BUT IT SHOULD NOT BE HAPPENING TO ME!! I truly thought that I was breaking the cycle. People! NO ONE SHOULD BE ABUSED! Not a man, not a woman, or a child! If you find that you are so angry that you feel the need to hit the person you claim you love, then you need to take your behind far away from them! Get away from the situation as fast as you can even if the other person does not want you to go GET AWAY and GET SOME HELP!!

Standing on my Healing: From Tainted to Chosen

So picture this scene with me: I am on the floor getting kneed in my head while everything is getting dark . I am feeling like I am losing consciousness. I need to do something to stop him or there is no telling what the outcome will be. I thought he loved me, I have known him since I was 14 years old, he was my high school sweetheart, we laughed together, we talked all the time, he asked to marry me and now he is kneeing me in my head with hatred felt blows! Wow my life! You never know how physically strong you are until you truly have to be. I had to get him off of me so with my bare hands and whatever strength I had I ripped his pants in the middle and begin twisting his balls like I was tried to bust them open. That got him off of me and gave me the opportunity to get up. I started punching and kicking on him until he got away from me and ran out of the house while snatching the phone from my daughter. I looked for a stick and as he came in the house I was trying to hit him with it and he ran back outside right when the police drove up. He was behind the cops with his clothes hanging off telling them I was crazy and trying to kill him. What? Really? I am crazy and trying to kill him?? I beg to differ!

While my dad and other family were pulling up the police tried to defuse the situation. All of my neighbors were outside and traffic was riding by slowly as they looked at the craziness coming from my house. I began to tell the cops that he had AIDS, he infected me with HIV and I was going to kill him! The police told me that I could be arrested for threatening him like that and I told them that if he came back in my house I was going to kill him. The police explained to me that I could not legally just put him out because we were married. I told them that if they leave and he came in then they may as well come back with the coroner because I would kill him! With a humorous look on their faces and a smirk the cops asked him if he had somewhere to go then asked me if he could put some clothes on. Even though I should not have allowed it, I let them escort him in with me watching as he got a few things and left with them. Once he left I bagged up his little bit of 'ish' and sat it outside. When I did that, the neighbors that were still outside began to clap!! Wow! I truly felt embarrassed about the chaos.

A few of them came over to check on me saying how nice I was, how mean he was when I was not around and that they were glad he was gone. My family wanted me to stay with them but I refused because I did not want him trying to get in my house while I was gone so they all stayed with me for a few hours. An hour or two goes by and as I am sitting in my living room my head started to hurt like crazy and I began to get light headed and dizzy. My family insisted that I go to the E.R. to get checked out so instead of refusing and so I went. After a few tests the doctor discovered that I had a severe concussion and the doctor advised me to rest. Well, despite the concussion, the physical, emotion, verbal, and mental hurt from the toxic union that I was in, I realized that I was now free! Or was I?

Reflection 24

"Wait! I Got Your Back!"

According to North Carolina Law you have to be legally separated for a year and it would take at least 6 months after that for a legal divorce. I really had to work on me! While I started to feel happy about no longer living in hell with a man God did not intend for me to be with in the first place, I was angry, depressed and extremely sad. I realized that I wanted revenge. Yes I know as a believer the bible reminds us **that "vengeance is mine says the Lord." (Deut. 32:35, Rom. 12:19, Heb.10:30)**, but in my state of mind I wanted that man dead!. I went to counseling sessions 3 days a week and even support groups. The counseling sessions forced me to look at me, in me, and around me. I was not just mad at the man I loved and trusted but I was especially angry with myself for not doing more to prevent what had occurred in my life. I felt totally out of place in the group meeting because people were explaining how they contracted the virus through drug use, risky behaviors and promiscuity. Well that was not me! I practiced abstinence, I waited for my husband and asked him if he had been tested for STDs, I thought I knew him - I thought I knew better but I found out that I was not this 'perfect' person I was trying to be. I was just like any other man or woman. I loved and I trusted but now I know that is not enough.

We as a people get so caught up in emotions that we do not ask enough questions; we fear rejection so we compromise, do not follow our inner instincts (listening to the voice of God) all for what we think is love and acceptance. As I speak to audiences I encourage others to ask

Standing on my Healing: From Tainted to Chosen

questions of those they are planning relationships with, get educated on sexually transmitted disease and infections, I explain to others the importance of knowing their status, the status of the person they are planning to be intimate with and to use protection. While many insist that abstinence is best, many do not abstain so it is very important to protect yourself and others. Advocates and sex educators explain the risks of not practicing abstinence, participating in risky behaviors and using protection. So with that said back to the story.

Everyone in the group was very nice. I was no different and certainly no better than anyone in there. We all had the same story just different scenarios - we were all HIV positive. Once I learned to forgive myself and get over myself I was able to truly love and accept people for who they are and not for what they do; besides that was not my place and who am I to judge. While attending counseling sessions and group sessions I also attempted to get my husband investigated to see if I had a case against him for what he did to me but it failed because I did not have any documented proof that showed he received a positive test before me in Philadelphia. So it was settled, it was time for me to set out a plan to kill him, and yes I was serious. Every day I would hear the "enemy" say, "Kill him!" but I would also hear God say "Wait I got your back".

Hearing both of the voices all the time made me feel as if I was going out of my mind while functioning like someone who had no personal problems at all. In the evening when my children went to sleep I would dress in dark clothes, get in my car and ride around town hoping that I would find him so that I could attack him and hopefully take his life. Did I know exactly what I was going to do? Did I truly think this thing through? No I did not, however, I did know

Standing on my Healing: From Tainted to Chosen

that the voices in my head kept telling me to kill him and those voices outweighed any positive thoughts I had at that time.

Those late night rendezvous were really draining. I was up late at night riding around the town like a crazy person, I was extremely exhausted while working and trying to concentrate on school was an understatement but most of all I was losing what was left of a relationship with my children as I lost who I was. I do not know how long I took part in those nightly shenanigans but eventually I became totally drained and numb. A few of my friends had been inviting me to a new church and since I had been out for so long as well as losing the connection with my children I decided to visit. I was too angry to go in the past and felt like I was not worthy to worship in the house of God because of the mistake I made with this man. Even though the people at the church were so nice I really did not want to go back but my children loved it. I had not seen them happy in a long time; they were the way children were supposed to be; happy, laughing and safe.

At first I could not understand why I had no desire to go after him anymore until January 2004 when I rededicated my life back to the Lord and got involved in a new church. While praying, praising and worshipping God told me that He was going to take care of everything and He had my back. Even though I did not fully understand it I had a peace in my heart. I had to move on with my life and I also knew that it was time to talk to my children because I did not want them to find out from other people or even from my family who knew what happened. Will my children be disgusted with me? Will they not love me anymore? Will they not want me

Standing on my Healing: From Tainted to Chosen

to touch them? Hug them? Cook for them? Will they be embarrassed? These are the question that ran through my mind and made me lose my breath. I could not hide it from them because I had people asking me to speak and my daughter was wondering why I kept taking them to "this AIDS place". Those were my daughter's words when I took them with me to Triad Heath Project (THP) on occasion which is the local agency who provides emotional and practical support to individuals living with HIV, to their loved ones and those at risk for HIV/AIDS. My daughter asked me one day, " Mommy why do we keep coming here? Do you have AIDS?". I said, "No, but how would you feel if I did?". She said," I do not know; I would be scared". That really let me know that it was time to talk to my babies.

Reflection 25

Release, It's Not About You!

As a parent you have to make the decision on when it is time to talk to your children about sexual education or any serious subject for that matter. As it pertained to me telling my children about my diagnosis there was never a good time, I just had to do it. The best way for me before I told them was to allow them to watch videos on the basics of HIV/AIDS, then we would do role plays about being pressured into sex. I allowed them to ask as many questions that they wanted and if I did not have the answer immediately then I would look it up for them. I really wanted my children to understand the importance of protecting themselves and how to protect themselves. I just wanted to protect my children and I hate this happened and was subjecting them to more hurt.

It was a Saturday afternoon and I decided to sit my children down to tell them. As soon as I had them sit down my daughter said, " Mommy I'm scared. Are you going to tell us bad news? Are you sick?". My eyes started to water so I took a deep breath to hold back the tears then I said, "Well, I have HIV." My son turned red, his eyes poured with tears and my daughter through her tears shouted, "HOW? WHEN? I know how but who did it? You do not have a boyfriend, you work all the time and go to school!". I proceeded to tell them where I contracted it. My babies broke down with tears and anger. It was harder telling them and seeing them cry than it was to get the diagnosis. I was so terrified after telling them but instead of rejection I

Standing on my Healing: From Tainted to Chosen

thought they would have toward me, they both hugged me and reassured me it would be alright. I do not know how long we cried together but I do know that the three of us became closer. I told them that I was healthy and despite the diagnosis, I would live a very long time. As a parent I had to be strong for my children because they were depending on me to care for them and to live.

After telling my children about the diagnosis I was then free to tell other members of my family and my friends. It really did not matter what people say or how they feel about your life decisions or circumstances, but it was important for me to tell my babies; besides God they are my life line. By law a person living with HIV is only required to tell their partners their status. Anyone else who knows are privileged to get that personal and transparent part of your life. You make the decision as to who and when you are ready to reveal that information. No one can put a time table on when or if you reveal your status. It is not an easy thing to do, therefore when you feel you are ready then you share the information. Some may accept you, some may shun you and some may have questions. You have to make up in your own mind how you will respond to their response(s), if at all. As for me, I chose to educate. I chose to educate those who accepted me, rejected me, laughed at me, gave me dirty looks, and those who loved me regardless. Educating others helped me to heal inside and out. Crying and embracing my fears, sadness and anger allowed me to heal inside and out. Receiving love and acceptance allowed me to heal inside and out. Receiving hugs allowed me to heal inside and out. Forgiving myself and loving myself allowed me to forgive, love and heal inside and out.

Standing on my Healing: From Tainted to Chosen

By the end of 2004 I forgave my ex-husband and that was the start of a new me. I went to a spiritual encounter with some of the ladies from church for the weekend and during the final night of the encounter all of the attendees were given a six inch nail with red paint on the end which was a symbolization of the nails that Jesus was pierced with. Once receiving the nail we walked up to the wooden cross and banged the nail in the cross as a symbolization of casting all of our cares, past hurts, and bondages on the cross. Honestly when I did that I felt free from my abusive step dad, the rape I experienced, the abortion I had, any hurts I inflicted on people, depression, sadness and the list goes on. I was totally healed from the hate and nothingness about myself that I once felt. God gave me the strength to forgive and healed me in the process and for that I continue to stand on my healing. **Isaiah 53:5 says that Jesus was wounded for our transgressions, bruised for our iniquities, the chastisement of our peace was upon Him and by His stripes I am healed;** I have been confessing that every day!

One day it really hit me that this situation or better yet this new life that I was living was not even about me but to help those on the same path. What can I do to help others who are already living with a diagnosis to live a happy, healthy and fulfilling life? I prayed about those questions that I had and God told me clearly to tell my story but this was not the answer that I was looking for; volunteering was not a problem but to stand in front of an audience telling them all of my traumatic experiences and allowing myself to be transparent and vulnerable- NO! Transparency and vulnerability got me where I am! Come on God, really!? I pondered what I heard in the spirit hoping that I would get something else but I always heard, "Tell your story". Everyone has a story, what makes me so different? So special? So unique? That is when God confirmed what I had in my spirit before; it is not about me.

Standing on my Healing: From Tainted to Chosen

During a community meeting for parents I spoke with a woman who connected me to Diane Robinson who was over the HIV/AIDS Community PROMISE Program at Piedmont Health Services and Sickle Cell Agency in Greensboro. PROMISE stands for Peers Reaching Out and Modeling Intervention Strategies whose purpose was to reduce the transmission of HIV/AIDS in high risk populations through skills building, counseling and risk reduction techniques. Ms Robinson aka Momma D, trained us, loved us, and protected us as we stood in front of audiences not only telling our stories but educating our community in the process. My first speaking engagement was at North Carolina Agricultural & Technical State University (A & T) in 2004 and man oh man was I terrified! I had always been very shy so the comments and looks on the student's faces as they walked in the sex education class was less than welcoming. Momma D set the tone by providing the basics on HIV/AIDS and even requesting respect toward us on the panel as we stood nervously yet boldly in front of the class. Before I even connected with anyone to do speaking engagements I used to have dreams of God showing me that I would be speaking in front of hundreds of people even someday writing a book. Well of course I told God that He was trippin' and there was no way that me of all people would be writing anything but a school paper let alone speaking in front of anyone! I must say, never underestimate the power of God and the gifts that He has created in you. You can only run so far and for so long.

Standing on my Healing: From Tainted to Chosen

HealedLee

One day while trying to find a filler for the void I my life I found God!

He helped me to forgive myself and then love myself.

Which has allowed me to freely love others

With that love I am an awesome daughter, sister, friend, woman and mother

Honestly…I am not 100% happy or complete

But am getting there by taking it a day at a time

Inside and out my Heavenly Father has healed me…which is why my name is HealedLee

Standing on my Healing: From Tainted to Chosen

Reflection 26

A Voice for the Voiceless

I was shaking inside, my palms were sweaty and my heart was racing but I took a deep breath, put my big girl panties on and started to speak. There were so many tears from not just me but from many in the audience also. I saw expressions of sadness, empathy, smiles and gratitude. When the class was over people came up for hugs and to thank us for sharing our personal lives with them. There were even some who said they had family members who were dealing with HIV/AIDS, have passed away from the affects of HIV/AIDS, or who themselves were nervous that they could have contracted the virus through unprotected sex. Needless to say many of the students got tested that day.

That day became one of many more opportunities to educate others. As a result of my transparency and bravery I have been privileged to share portions of my story on college campuses, the local news, in local newspapers and magazines, as well as on blog talk radio shows. I have also become a member of several organizations who advocate for persons living with HIV. There are so many leadership and advocacy opportunities I have been able to partake in which I do not mention this to brag, but instead to share my victories over the adversities in my life. God has given me so much grace and I am humbled and grateful for where He has bought me from. Without God's unchanging hand I would not be where I am now or have come this far. I did not allow a negative diagnosis to tear me down but instead I allowed God to use me

Standing on my Healing: From Tainted to Chosen

to use my voice to be a voice for the voiceless in the way of sharing my experiences and achievements.

In 2007, I received my Associate's degree in Social Work from Guilford Technical Community College. In 2009, I receive my Bachelor's degree in Social Work from the University of North Carolina at Greensboro. In 2014 I received my Master's in Public Health from Capella University and I am currently completing my doctorate degree in Public Health also at Capella University. Why am I sharing this? I am sharing this because I could have allowed the trials and tribulation in my life to beat me down and keep me down. I could have become a product of the things that happened to me but instead I decided that I was not going to look like or be like what I have been through. I pressed on regardless to how hard it seemed. The harder things got, the harder I knew I had to work. Was it easy? Of course not! There were times that I felt I was 5 steps ahead then I got pushed 10 steps back BUT GOD!!

Standing on my Healing: From Tainted to Chosen

I did not do any of this alone either, people came into my life for a reason and for a season. I learned from them whether it was good or bad. My children definitely kept me afloat. I was not the best mom they could have had but I did the best that I could and they strengthened me in the process. Some of my family pushed me, loved me, accepted and encouraged me. My friends laughed with me, cried with me, cursed with me, fussed with me and at me, they also pushed me to be better, they encouraged me to press forward and never give up. Everyone told me that people are waiting for my story, they are waiting for me.

I encourage everyone who reads this to never give up on you dreams. Set goals. Do not worry about what people say because someone will always find something to say. Do not try to be like anyone except who God created you to be. When He made you He broke the mold because you are unique, you are fearfully and wonderfully made! Speak life over your situations and know that trouble does not last always. God has bigger and better things for you and your best is yet to come! Learn to love who you are by building a relationship with God through conversation and hearing of the word. God is not mad at you but He is madly in love with you!

Standing on my Healing: From Tainted to Chosen

In communing with Him and trusting Him, He will show you just how much He really loves you and then empower you to begin to love and forgive others. Now that I know who I am and Whose I am I truly know that I am God's Favorite Daughter, I know that I am not dirty or tainted but instead I am chosen. I am chosen to be a light in a dark place for someone else. I am standing on my healing because I am HealedLee and I know that I Will Live!

When I finished writing my book I cried tears of joy because I have been writing it since 2008. While I was finishing up my book my brother was really sick and we the family knew he was not going to last much longer. I wanted to make sure that I finished this book before he passed so that I could read it to him. The day that I planned to read it to my big bro, he passed away. It was Monday July 13, 2015 at 1:30pm. I was not ready; none of us were ready. You cannot ever be ready or prepared for the passing of a loved one. I physically lost my best friend that day and it felt like I had a major organ removed, but I know he will forever be a part of me. After his funeral I realized that he was in me and I in him which means he knows every word in this book. I miss my brother dearly and I dedicate every accomplishment to him. I am determined to keep making him proud of me. He will forever be my Ace, my Pea in a Pod, my Broheim!

Standing on my Healing: From Tainted to Chosen

Standing on my Healing: From Tainted to Chosen

Standing on my Healing: From Tainted to Chosen

A Letter 'Cause You're Gone by *Walter 'June' Shepherd Jr.*

I wonder will this poem even measure up to the person it's for?

The smile, the laugh, the feeling, and allure?

The energy, the presences, the unspoken evidence?

The words of wisdom that seem to be heaven sent.

No dying flower can replace my undying love.

Like no dying star can replace the sun up above.

Still my mind is playing tricks on me: through my eyes you are gone.

But my heart doesn't understand.

Cause through it you live on.

So my mind has to choose between what I see and what I feel.

Then I hear your voice and I know your love is still very real

Written by Walter "June" Shepherd Jr. 7/25/2015©

Standing on my Healing: From Tainted to Chosen

Thank You

Mom, Mother, Ma, Mommy!! I thank you for loving me, for raising me to the best of your ability and for reminding me how beautiful, how wonderful and needed I am!!

Dad, Daddy, Popadopolis!! Thank you for being the father I truly needed in my life and for always supporting me through everything. I love you so much!

Tamara, Tamika and Shauntaya: Tameeeerrrrr, Meekee, and Tayyyyderr!! I love you guys for life for always being great support systems, for loving me and taking this journey of sisterhood life with me!! You three are my true blood sisters, my ride or die!

My beautiful Charisma and my handsome Amir!! My darling children! I could not have gotten this far without you both in my life. I know things in our life have not been the best but I thank you for sticking it out with me and being 2 of the best children anyone could have ever asked for. I love you guys forever and ever!

Diane Robinson aka Momma D: I truly believe in my heart that I would not have broken through my fear of public speaking had it not been for you. You molded me, encouraged me and protected me as I grew to be the advocate and educator that I am. You have made such a difference in the lives of so many, you are truly loved and appreciated.

Pastors Lee & Shonia you guys are the best spiritual parents in the world to me! You said to give you three years and my life would be changed for the better, well that was 14 years ago and I am in awe of God's grace and favor on my life. Thank you for pouring into my life the unadulterated Word of God. I love you both and my Destiny family!

Pastors Omar & Brandi Rojas and DYmondFYre Global Publishing for believing in me, taking a chance on me, and encouraging me throughout this process.

Tina Wright, Shannon King and Stevii Mills: You ladies are my rock! Words cannot express the love I have for each of you. Through the tears, the fussing I did, the late night calls, the laughs, the prayers, the dinners, etc. you ladies were always there through every single step I made to complete this journey. For that and much more I say thank you!

Thank you Okeeze Artography, Derek Palmer Photography and L.A. Photography for bringing art to my life through camera with your beautiful gift!

To the countless people in my life, friends and family: There are too many of you to name and I do not want to miss anyone. Many of you encouraged me, prayed with me, prayed for me and pushed me hard. For that I say thank you!

Standing on my Healing: From Tainted to Chosen

Standing on my Healing: From Tainted to Chosen

Sources:

AIDS.gov. 2014. www.aids.gov

American Cancer Society, Inc. 2014. www.cancer.org

American Diabetes Association. (1995-2016). What is gestational diabetes? Retrieved from http://www.diabetes.org/diabetes-basics/gestational/what-is-gestational-diabetes.html#sthash.KCCr4a42.dpuf

Center for Disease Control and Prevention. 2014. www.cdc.gov

DeSisto CL, Kim SY, Sharma AJ. Prevalence Estimates of Gestational Diabetes Mellitus in the United States, Pregnancy Risk Assessment Monitoring System (PRAMS), 2007–2010. Prev Chronic Dis 2014;11:130415. DOI:http://dx.doi.org/10.5888/pcd11.130415

John Carroll University. (n.d.) Stalking statistics. www.sites.jcu.edu/pages/stalking/stalking-statistics/

Merriam-Webster (n.d). Charisma. Retrieved from www.merriam-webster.com/dictionary/charisma

Piedmont Health Services and Sickle Cell Agency. 2005. http://www.piedmonthealthservices.org/

Triad Health Project. 2015. http://www.triadhealthproject.com/

Connect with the Author

We are grateful for your support on this project! Connect with Author Alicia E. Diggs by visiting the following:

Facebook:

https://www.facebook.com/pages/I-Will-Live/387660567980886?ref=hl

Blogspot:

http://iwilllive-healedlee/blogspot.com/

Made in the USA
Columbia, SC
23 January 2020